Gujarat Road Atlas
& STATE DISTANCE GUIDE

2008

Editors :
Dr. R. P. Arya
Jitender Arya
Dr. Gayathri Arya
Anshuman Arya

CONTENTS

LEGENDS

——— International Boundary	★ Tourist Place
—·—·— State Boundary	▬▬▬ National Express Highway
— — — District Boundary	▬▬▬ Golden Quadrilateral
▬▬▬ Railway Line	▬▬▬ East - West Corridor
▣ State Capital	▦8▦ National Highway With No.
✪ District Hqtrs.	▬▬▬ Major Road
◉ Taluk Hqtrs.	——— Other Road
• Other Town	✈ Aerodrome / Airlines
～ River	◉ Jain Pilgrim Centre

IMS ®

Designed, Cartographed, Printed & Published by :

INDIAN MAP SERVICE इण्डियन मैप सर्विस

Sector 'G', Shastri Nagar, Near Ram Mandir, Jodhpur - 3 (Raj.) INDIA
Tel. : 2612871, 2612872, 2612873, 2612874, Fax : (0291) 2612870
Email : indianmapservice@yahoo.co.in, indianmap@satyam.net.in

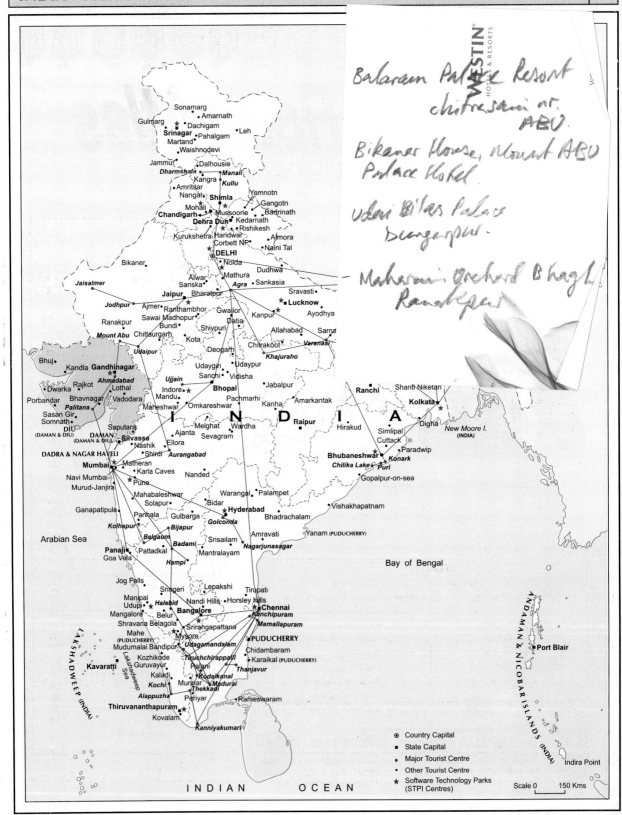

Handwritten notes:

Balaram Palace Resort
chitresani nr.
ABU.

Bikaner House, Mount ABU
Palace Hotel.

Udai Bilas Palace
Dungarpur.

– Maharani Orchard Bhagh
Ranakpur

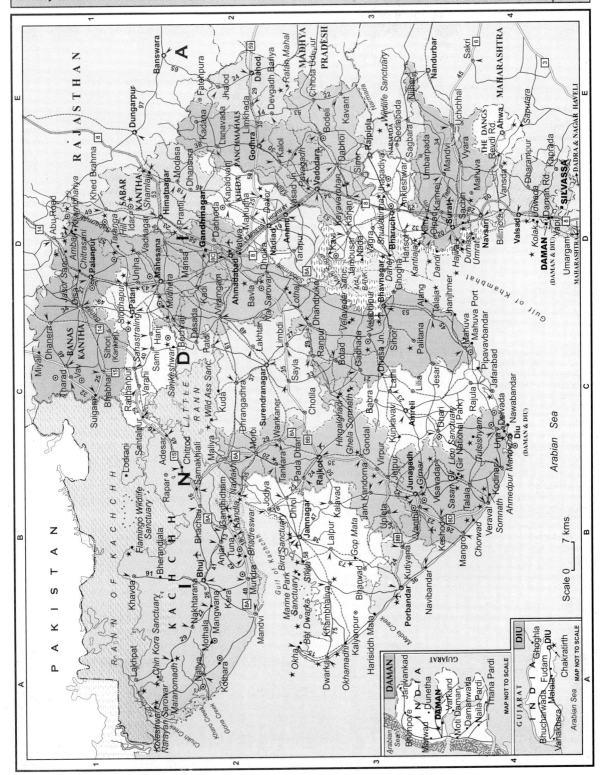

Welcome to.....

GUJARAT

Gorgeous Gujarat, the `glorious land' of India has a very rich historical and cultural legacy. It gets the name from "Gujjar Rashtra", the land of Gujjars, a migrant tribe who came to India in the wake of the invading Huns in 5th century. The State is dotted with several Harappan sites, dating back to 2nd century B.C. The region came under the reigns of various dynasties like Mauryas, Guptas, Pratiharas etc., but it was during the rule of Chalukyas (Solankis) that the State witnessed great progress and prosperity. During this time Gujarat was attacked and plundered by the rampaging forces of Mahmud of Ghazni, but the Chalukyan kings were able to maintain general prosperity and well being of the State. After this glorious respite, the region faced troubled times under the Muslims, Marathas and the British. Gujarat also played a very important role in India's struggle for freedom. Mohandas Karamchand Gandhi, the most illustrious son of the State and the "father of the nation", gave a new direction to the movement of freedom struggle. Some of the other stalwarts of the freedom movement from Gujarat are Dadabhai Naoroji, Pherozshah Mehta, Badruddin Tayabji, Vithalbhai Patel and Sardar Vallabhbhai Patel etc. Gujarat, is also regarded as a bastion of Jainism. Jains, a thriving mercantile society well known for their business acumen and enterprise have contributed a lot in the progress of the State. The State has witnessed a spectacular growth in every sector and is one of the leading industrialised States of India, with industrial giants like Tata, Reliance etc. hailing from this land. Gujarat has also emerged as a leading tourist destination in the country. The rich history and culture as well as the immense natural beauty and charm provides a fabulous off-beat holiday. Its numerous archaeological and historical sites, majestic monuments, sacred sites, 1666 kms. long coastline dotted with excellent beaches, hill and health resorts, wildlife sanctuaries, handicrafts, cuisine and a tradition of hospitality combined with excellent transport network and other modern amenities will compel any traveller to pack the bags and reach for this amazing destination.

PLACES OF INTEREST

AHMADABAD : Amazing Ahmadabad, teeming with splendid monuments, mosques, pavilions and mausoleums is a fine blend of ancient heritage and vibrant present. Originally, a township named as Karnavati was founded by King Karna Solanki in 1063 - 1093, on the banks of river Sabarmati. The present city was built by Sultan Ahmed Shah in 1411, on the ruins of Karnavati. Sir Thomas Roe, the British envoy to Jehangir's court, was so impressed by the glory of Ahmadabad that he referred it as "the handsomest town in Hindustan, perhaps in the world". The city became an important textiles centre and was referred as the "Manchester of the East". Today, this `Gateway to Gujarat' is the largest city in the State and is also the commercial and cultural nerve centre of Gujarat.

Shaking Minarets - These two unique minarets at the Siddhi Bashir mosque are the most popular monuments of the city. The three storeyed minarets are girdled by carved stone balconies and are designed in a way that when one minaret is shaken the other one vibrates too.

Jumma Masjid - The mosque is located in the centre of the old city and was built by Sultan Ahmed Shah in 1423.

Siddi Saiyad Mosque - The beautiful mosque built in Indo-Saracenic Style lies near the Lal Darwaza and is world renowned for its exquisite stone window tracery.

Rani Rupmati Mosque - It was built in 1430 - 1440, by the Hindu wife of Sultan Mehmud Beghara.

Rani Sipri's Mosque - It was built in 1514, by Rani Sipri, a queen of Mehmud Begarha. The mosque is an architectural masterpiece and perhaps the most beautiful monument in the city.

Rauza of Shah Alam - The exquisite tomb and mosque commemorates a Muslim saint Shah Alam. It was built by Asaf Khan, the brother of Mughal empress Nur Jehan.

Hatheesing Temple - The Jain temple dedicated to Lord Dharmnath, the 15th *tirthankar* was built in 1848, by Shri Kesarisimha Hatheesing Shah. It is known for exquisite carvings on white marble. 52 small shrines surround the spacious courtyard.

Bhadra Fort - The foundation of the fort was laid in 1411. Within its bastions were royal palaces and gardens. A chamber here was converted into the Bhadra Kali temple by the Marathas.

Gandhi Ashram - It was setup by Gandhiji in 1915 on the banks of river Sabarmati, about 7 kms. north of the city. The humble *ashram* became the beacon of freedom struggle. Hriday Kunj, the simple cottage of the Mahatama is today a national monument and houses a small museum. A sound and light spectacle based on Mahatma's life is held here in the evenings.

Sabarmati Ashram   *Shaking Minarets*   *Siddi Saiyad Mosque*   *Hatheesing Temple*

Kankaria Lake - This beautiful polygonal lake was built by Sultan Qutb-ud-Din in 1451. Amidst the lake is an island-garden with a summer palace known as Nagina Wadi.

Calico Textile Museum - This unique museum houses a rich and rare collection of antique textiles from 17th century onwards.

Sarkhej Roza - It is about 8 kms. from the city and is known for the elegant architectural complexes. The important buildings are — tomb of Ahmed Khattu Ganj Baksh, the mosque, the tombs of Mehmud Shah Begada and his queen and the palace and pavilions, built around the tank of Sarkhej.

AROUND AHMADABAD

Adalaj Vav (19 kms.) - The famous step well (*vav*)is located on the outskirts of Adalaj village and was built in 1499, by Queen Rudabai. The intricately carved step well is built several stories in depth and is a unique specimen of architecture.

Gandhinagar (25 kms.) - The capital city of Gujarat is the second planned modern city of India. The State Government complex lies at the centre around which are thirty self-sufficient sectors.

Akshardham - This architectural wonder of 20th century is one the most famous temples of the Swaminarayan sect. It sprawls across an area of 23 acres and the main shrine stands 108 feet tall amidst lush green lawns. About 6,000 tonnes of pink sandstone was used to create this giant edifice and no steel or any metal was used in the building. The shrine houses a marvellously sculpted 7 ft. high gold leafed statue of Lord Swami Narayan. There is also an amusement park, a museum, picture gallery and library.

AHMEDPUR MANDVI : It is one of the finest beaches of the country. Across the resort is Diu, which can be reached by a ferry or a bridge connecting the island.

AMBAJI & KUMBHARIA : It is one of the most important pilgrim centres of Gujarat. The famous shrine of Goddess Ambaji atop Arasur hill is considered to be one of the `Shakti Peeth's. Nearby are famous Kumbharia Jain temples noted for their ornate beauty.

BHAVNAGAR : It was founded by Bhavsinhji Gohil in 1743 and is a flourishing port on the Gulf of Khambhat.

Places of attraction - **Gaurishankar Lake, Takhteswar Temple and Burton Museum** etc.

BHUJ : This "Jewel of the Kachchh" was the capital of the former princely State of Kutch.

Aina Mahal - This beautiful Indian palace with European influence was built in 1759, by Rao Lakhpatji.

Prag Mahal - This imposing palace was made by Rao Paragmalji II. It is built in Italian Gothic style and has a large Darbar Hall, big rooms, wide verandahs and a 45 metre high bell tower.

Kachchh Museum - The museum located on the banks of Hamirsar lake was established in 1877, by Maharao Khengarji III and is the oldest museum of Gujarat.

CHORWAD : It is the only 'Palace Beach Resort' in India.

DAKOR : It is the second most sacred town after Dwarka for the devotees of Lord Krishna.

DWARKA : The abode of Lord Krishna is one of the "Char Dhams" of Hindu pilgrimage. It is said that Lord Krishna settled and established his kingdom here after leaving Mathura. It is also a fine beach resort.

Dwarkadhish (Jagat Mandir) - This sacred temple of Lord Krishna is an excellent architectural monument. The shrine consists of Nij Mandir and a multipillared Sabha Griha, that leads to the main sanctum, which is said to be 2,500 years old. A conical spire atop the temple rises upto 157 m. that dominates the skyline.

Nageshwar Mahadev - It is 17 kms. from Dwarka and enshrines one of the twelve *jyotirlingas* of Lord Shiva.

Girnar Hill - The sacred hill is an important pilgrim centre for Hindus, Jains and Muslims. The first set of Jain temples are at a height of 610 m., the main temple is dedicated to Lord Neminath. The shrines of Ambaji, Gorakhnath and Guru Dattatraya are further up on the sacred mount. On the top there is a shrine dedicated to Shiva and a *Dargah*.

DUMAS : An excellent sea-side resort, about 16 kms. from Surat.

HAJIRA : This industrial capital of South Gujarat and beautiful beach resort lies 28 kms. from Surat.

JAMNAGAR : It was founded by Jam Raval in 1540 and was the capital of the former princely state of Navanagar. The town is also known as "Chhoti Kashi".

Lakhota Palace & Tank - This scenic site is a popular picnic spot. The fortified palace set in the centre of the lake can be reached by an arched stone bridge.

Solarium or Ranjit Institute of Poly Radio Therapy - The centre was established in 1933 by Jam Ranjitsinhji and was one of the three such medical centres in the world during that time.

JUNAGADH : It lies at the foothills of the sacred Girnar hill and is resplendent with mythological legends. The antiquity of the city dates back to pre-Harappan times and was ruled by Mauryas, Kshatrapas, Guptas, Vallabhis, Chudasamas, Gujarat Sultans and Babi Nawabs.

Uparkot or Upper Fort - This stronghold of Mauryas and Guptas has survived about 16 sieges in last 1000 years. The fort wall around the town and fort made Uparkot virtually inaccessible.

Akshardham Temple	*Ambaji Temple*	*Women of Kachchh*	*Dwarkadhish Temple*

Maqbaras - The mausoleums of the Nawabs of Junagadh are a fine representation of *Nawabi* architecture.

Ashoka's Rock Edict - A huge boulder inscribed with 14 edicts of emperor Ashoka (257-56 B.C) lie on the way to Girnar from Uparkot. **The temples of Girnar -** The holy hill of Girnar is adorned with several intricately carved and sculpted shrines of Hindus and Jains. The Mahashivratri fair held here is attended by *Naga sadhus* and pilgrims from all over India.

KOTESHWAR : Ancient Hindu pilgrim centre known for the Mahadev temple, set on a high plinth overlooking the sea. The sacred Narayan Sarovar lake is located nearby.

LOTHAL : It was an important port town of the Harappan era, dating back to 2nd century BC. A well planned city was discovered under the mound near Saragwala village in 1954. The mound was called Lothal, which means dead in the local dialect.

MODHERA : It is famous for the ancient Sun Temple, which is one of the most magnificent monuments of Gujarat and the best example of Solanki temple architecture. The ornately carved temple was built in 1026 - 27 AD., by Bhimadev I and was later destroyed by Mahmud of Ghazni. Adjacent to the temple is a huge 'Sun Kund' (Rama Kund) surrounded by step-terraces with 108 smaller Shrines.

PATAN : This Jain and Hindu pilgrim centre was a great centre of art, culture, literature and education under the Solankis. The town is dotted with several Jain and Shaivite shrines. The Shastraling Lake, built by King Siddhraj Jaising is surrounded by 1000 Shiva temples. It is also renowned as Patola weaving centre.

PORBANDAR : This birth place of Mahatma Gandhi was an ancient port town. The present day town was established by Rana Sartanji in 1785 and is noted for its town planning and architecture.

Gandhiji's House & Kirti Mandir - Gandhiji was born in 1869, at his ancestral house over here. Today, it is a national monument and open for public viewing. The adjacent house, called as Kirti Mandir has a Gandhian library and a prayer hall.

Sudama Mandir - It is the only temple dedicated to Sudama, the childhood friend of Lord Krishna.

RAJKOT : It was founded in the 16th century by Kunvar Vibhoji Jadeja and was the capital of the princely state of Saurashtra. Rajkot is known for its handicrafts like applique work, bead and mirror work, tie and dye (bandhni) and gold and silver jewellery.

Karba Gandhi no Delo - It is Gandhiji's ancestral home and now houses Gandhi Smriti, a permanent exhibition.

Watson Museum & Library - The museum at the charming Jubilee gardens displays the cultural heritage of Saurashtra.

Jagat Mandir - It is dedicated to Shri Ramkrishna Parmahansa.

Rajkumar College - It was built in 1870 and is one of the oldest public schools of India. **Lal Pari Lake & Randerda -** This picturesque spot 5 kms. from Rajkot is a popular picnic spot.

AROUND RAJKOT

Wankaner - It is about 50 kms. from Rajkot and is famous for the Wankaner Palace, which has been converted into a heritage hotel.

SURAT : This flourishing port city on the banks of river Tapti is one of the oldest trading centres of India. It is renowned for fine silks, exquisite brocades and trade in spices. The British East India Company established its first ware houses in Surat in 1612.

Old Fort - It was built by Mohammed Tughlak in the 14th century as a defence fortification against the Bhils. **Rangupavan -** It is one of the biggest open air theatre in the country. The theatre has a capacity of 4,000. **Sardar Patel Museum -** The old museum has a rich collection of over 10,000 specimens of arts and crafts. **Textile Market -** It is India's major centre of textile trade.

SAPUTARA : Saputara, literally the 'Abode of the Serpent' is perched at an altitude of 1,000 meters in the heart of the Dangs district. It is known for cool bracing climate as well as scenic views of the verdant valleys. Saputara has been developed as a planned hill resort, studded with all modern amenities.

SASAN GIR SANC. : It is 54 kms. from Junagarh and covers an area of 500 sq. miles. The sanctuary is the famous home of Asiatic Lion. Other animals here are - bear, antelope, fox, black buck etc.

SHAMLAJI : The exquisitely carved shrine houses the idol of Shamlaji made in black stone.

SOMNATH : Somnath, the shrine eternal is considered to be as old as creation. Like a phoenix, the temple has risen seven times from ashes and depicts a saga of devotion and heroism. The legendary temple is believed to have been built by the Moon God - Soma and enshrines first of the 12 *jyotirlingas*. The present temple structure was commissioned by Sardar Patel in 1950's.

PALITANA : One of the most important Jain pilgrim centres is located 58 kms. from Bhavnagar. The sacred Shatrunjaya hill has 863 magnificent temples which were built over an impressive span of 900 years.

TITHAL : This popular holiday resort dotted with palm sheltered cottages lies 5 kms. from Valsad.

TULSI SHYAM : This enchanting pilgrim site near Junagadh (128 kms.) is known for hot springs and temple dedicated to Bhim and his mother Kunti.

Modhera Sun Temple *Lion, Sasan Gir* *Mahabat Maqbara, Junagadh*

UBHARAT : The sandy beach with a backdrop of shady palm groves was the summer resort of the Gaekwads of Vadodara. Long beaches at Ubharat are very popular among tourists. It is 40 kms. from Surat.

VADODARA : This graceful city of magnificent palaces, museums, splendid temples, graceful gardens, shady avenues and many world renowned institutions of learning is perhaps the de-facto cultural capital of Gujarat. It served as the capital of princely Gaekwads, the rule of Sayajirao Gaekwad III (1885 - 1920), a great patron of art and learning is said to be the golden era of Vadodara. Today, the city on the banks of river Vishwamitri is a thriving industrial and commercial centre and is also regarded as the industrial capital of Gujarat'.

Vadodara Museum & Picture Gallery - It was founded by Sayajirao III in 1894 and is one of the finest museums in Asia.

Maharaja Sayajirao University - This prestigious university was founded by Maharaja Sayajirao in 1840. The campus is noted for its architectural grandeur.

Sayaji Baug - Public garden with an excellent zoo.

Nazarbaugh Palace - It was built in 1721 and is noted for the 'Sheesh Mahal' or mirror palace made in old classical style.

Kirti Mandir - This family vault of the Gaekwads is decorated with murals made by Nandlal Bose.

Dakshinamoorthy Temple - It was constructed by EME school in the cantonment area. The temple dedicated to Lord Shiva is set amidst five banyan trees and is unique in concept and design.

Some other places of interest are — Tambekar Wada, ISCKON Temple, Clock Tower, Khanderao Market, Sursagar Lake, Tapovan Complex etc.

AROUND VADODARA

Ajwa & Nimeta (20kms.) - The twin gardens here are designed on the pattern of famous Brindavan Gardens of Mysore. There is also an amusement park and resort nearby.

Anand (35 kms.) - The world renowned Anand milk co-operative or Amul is located here. It is the perhaps most successful co-operative movements of its kind and has put India among the list of major milk producers of the world.

Champaner (47 kms.) - It was founded by Mahmud Shah Begada in 1484 and was the political capital of Gujarat till 1536. The site was abandoned 300 years ago and has ruins of numerous palaces and mosques built in Indo - Saracenic style.

FAIRS & FESTIVALS CALENDAR

Month	Fair/Festival	Place	Famous For
Jan./Feb.	MakarSankranti	Ahmadabad	Kite flying festival
Feb./Mar.	Bhavnath Mahadeo,	Mount Girnar	Folk music and bhajans
	Shivratri Fair	Junagadh distt.	
Mar./Apr.	Holi	All over Gujarat	Festival of colours
	Dangs Darbar	Dangs distt.	Tribal dance & music
	Chitra Vichitra	Gumbhakhari (Sabarkantha)	Colourful celebrations, tribal culture and costumes
	Madhavrai Fest.	Madhavpura	Lord Krishna's marriage Anniv.
	Shah Alam Fair	Ahmadabad	Held in the memory of Muslim saint Shah Alam
	Mahavir Jayanti	Palitana	Lord Mahavir's birth anniversary
Jul./Aug.	Sarkhej Fair	Sarkhej	Largest Muslim fair
	Rath Yatra	Ahmadabad	Huge procession of Lord Krishna, Balram & Subhadra
	Pateti	Udwada	New year day of Parsi's
	Janamashtami	Dwarka & Dakor	Lord Krishna's birth anniversary
Aug./Sept	Tarnetar Fair	Tarnetar	Husband hunt tribal festival.
	Navratri	All over Gujarat	Most colourful & prominent event
	Dussehra	All over Gujarat	Signifies victory over evil
Oct./Nov.	Diwali	All over Gujarat	Festival of Lights
	Vautha Fair	Vautha	One of the biggest in the State
	Siddhpur Fair	Siddhpur	Camel bazaar is organised
	Somnath Mahadev Fair	Somnath	Birth celebrations of Lord Shiva's son Kartikeya
	Shamalaji Fair	Shamalaji	3 week long celebrations
	Pavagadh Fair	Pavagadh	Sacrifices & yagnas held to propitiate Goddess Kali
	Swaminarayan Fair	Gadhada	

Somnath Temple

Samavaran Temple, Palitana

High Court, Vadodara

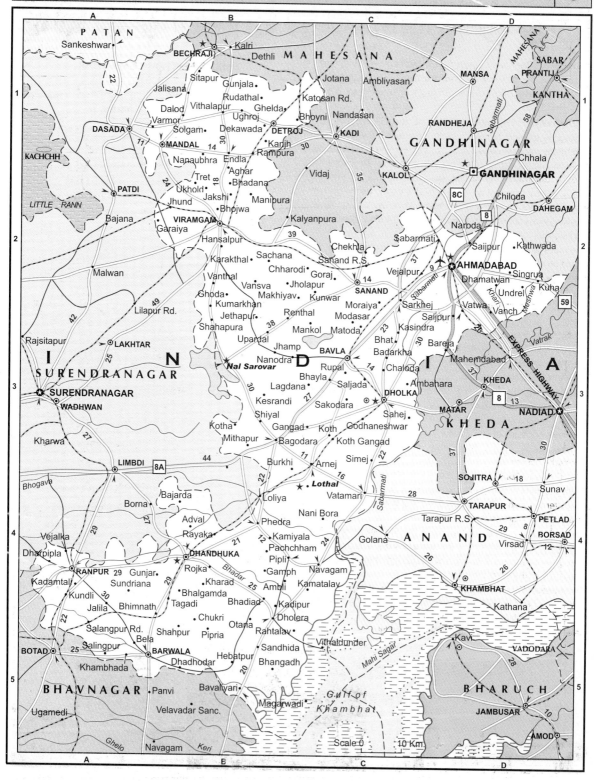

PATAN

Sankeshwar

22

Jalisana · Sitapur · Gunjala

BECHRAJI · Kalri

Dethli · MAHESANA

Jotana · Ambliyasan

MANSA

SABAR

PRANTIJ

Rudathal · Ghelda · Katosan Rd.

Vithalapur · Ughroj · Bhoyni · Nandasan

Dalod · Varmor · Solgam · Dekawada · DETROJ · KADI

DASADA · Kanjh · Rampura

MANDAL · 14 · Endla · Aghar

KACHCHH · Nanaubhra · Bhadana

Tret · Bhojwa · Manipura

Ukhold · Jakshi

Jhund

LITTLE RANN

PATDI

Bajana

Garaiya · VIRAMGAM

Hansalpur

Karakthal · Sachana

Malwan

Vanthal · Chharodi

Ghoda · Vansva · Makhiyav

Kumarkhan · Jethapur · Renthal

Lilapur Rd.

Shahapura

Upardal

Rajsitapur

LAKHTAR

SURENDRANAGAR

SURENDRANAGAR

WADHWAN

Kharwa

LIMBDI · 8A · 44

Bhogavo

Borna · Bajarda

Adval

Vejalka · Rayaka

Dharpipla

RANPUR · 29 · Gunjar

Kadamtali · Sundriana

Kundli · Jalila · Bhimnath

Salangpur Rd. · Bela

BOTAD · 25 · Salingpur · BARWALA

Khambhada · Dhadhodar

BHAVNAGAR · Panvi

Ugamedi · Velavadar Sanc.

Ghelo · Navagam · Keri

GANDHINAGAR

RANDHEJA

KALOL

8C · Chiloda

8 · DAHEGAM

Naroda

Sabarmati · Saijpur · Kathwada

AHMADABAD

Dhamatwan · Singrua

Vejalpur · Sarkhej · Undrel · Kuha

Saijpur · Vatwa · Vanch · 59

Kasindra

Bhat · Bareja

Badarkha

Mahemdabad

KHEDA

8 · 13

MATAR · NADIAD

KHEDA

Ambahara

SOJITRA · 18

Sunav

TARAPUR

Tarapur R.S · PETLAD

29 · BORSAD

Virsad · 12

ANAND

26

KHAMBHAT

Kathana

VADODARA

JAMBUSAR · 10

AMOD

Scale 0 · 10 Km

Gulf of Khambhat

BHARUCH

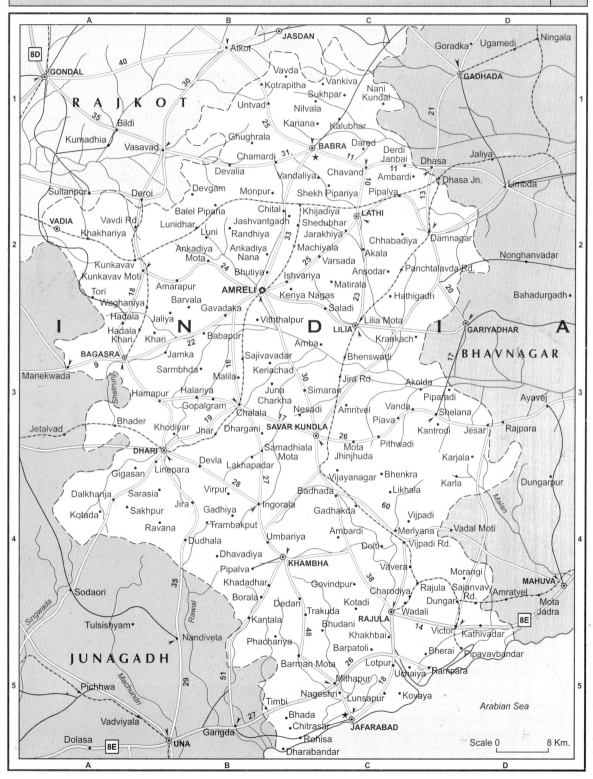

AMRELI

8D

GONDAL

RAJKOT

JASDAN

Atkot

Vavda

Kotrapitha

Vankiva

Nani Kundal

Goradka · Ugamedi · Ningala

GADHADA

Untvad

Nilvala

Sukhpar

Bildi

35

Kumadhia

Vasavad

Ghughrala

Kariana · Kalubhar

Dared

Derdi Janbai

Dhasa

Jaliya

21

Chamardi 31

BABRA

11

11

Dhasa Jn.

Limbda

13

Devalia

Chavand

Ambardi

Sultanpur

Deroi

Devgam

Monpur

Vandaliya

Shekh Pipariya

Pipalva

VADIA

Balel Piparia

Chital

Khijadiya

LATHI

Damnagar

Nonghanvadar

Vavdi Rd.

Lunidhar

Jashvantgadh

Shedubhar

Chhabadiya

Khakhariya

Luni

Randhiya

Jarakhiya

Akala

Balel

Ankadiya Mota

Ankadiya Nana

Machiyala

Varsada

Ansodar

Panchtalavda Rd.

20

Bahadurgadh

Kunkavav

Kunkavav Moti

Bhutiya

Ishvariya

Matirala

Hathigadh

Tori

Amarapur

AMRELI

Keriya Nagas

Saladi

Waghaniya

Barvala

Gavadaka

Viththalpur

Lilia Mota

GARIYADHAR

Hadala

Jaliya

LILIA

Krankach

BHAVNAGAR

Hadala Khari

Khari

22

Babapur

Amba

17

BAGASRA

Jamka

Sajivavadar

Bhenswadi

9

Sarmbhda

Malila

Keriachad

Jira Rd.

Akolda

Manekwada

Halariya

Juna Charkha

Simaran

Piparadi

Ayavej

Hamapur

Nesadi

Amritvel

Vanda

Shelana

Bhader

Gopalgram

19

Chalala 17

Dhargani

SAVAR KUNDLA

Piava

Kantrodi

Jesar

Rajpara

Jetalvad

Khodiyar

Jhar

26

Mota Jhinjhuda

Pithwadi

Karjala

Dungarpur

DHARI

Devla

Lakhapadar

Samadhiala Mota

27

Karla

Gigasan

Linepara

28

Virpur

Vijayanagar

Bhenkra

Likhala

Dalkhanja

Sarasia

Jira

Gadhiya

Ingorala

Badhada

60

Vijpadi

Merlyana

Vadal Moti

Kotada

Sakhpur

Trambakput

Gadhakda

Ambardi

Vijpadi Rd.

MAHUVA

Ravana

Dudhala

Umbariya

Dolth

Vavera

Morangi

Mota Jadra

Dhavadiya

KHAMBHA

Govindpur

Charodiya

Rajula

Sajanvav Rd.

Amratvel

8E

Pipalva

Khadadhar

38

Kotadi

Dungar

Wadali

14

Victor

Kathivadar

Sodaori

Borala

Dedan

Trakuda

RAJULA

Bherai

Pipavavbandar

Tulsishyam

Kantala

Bhudani

Khakhbai

Nandivela

Phachariya

Barpatoli

Lotpur

Uchaiya

Rampara

Pichhwa

26

Barman Mota

18

Koyaya

Timbi

Nageshri

Mithapur

Lunsapur

Arabian Sea

Vadviyala

27

Bhada

Chitrasar

JAFARABAD

Dolasa

UNA

Gangda

Rohisa

8E

Dharabandar

Scale 0   8 Km.

JUNAGADH

29

51

35

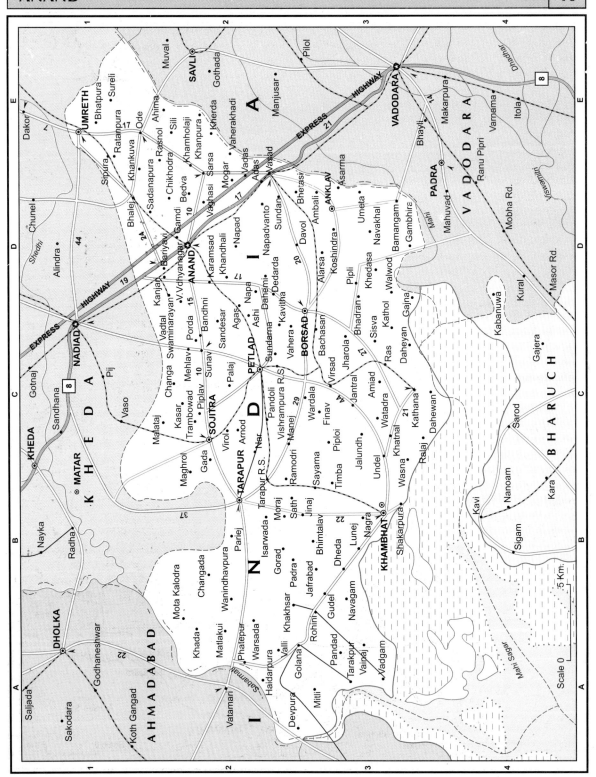

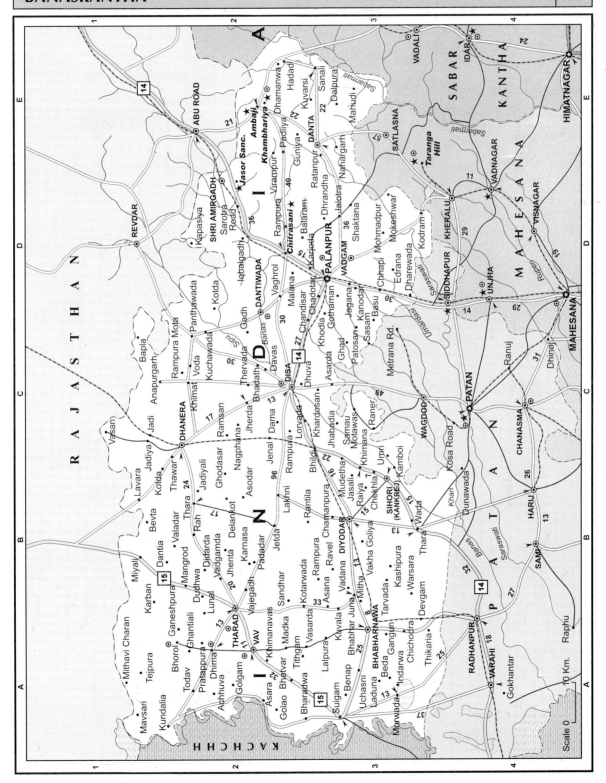

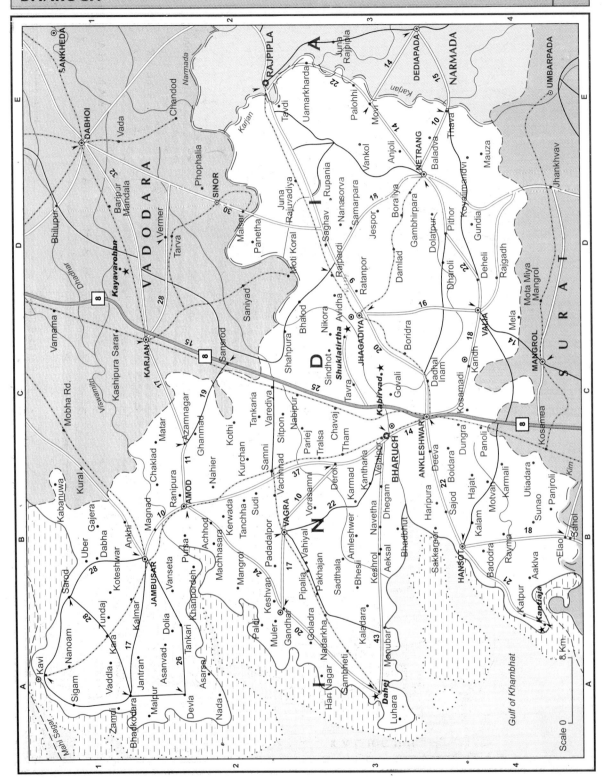

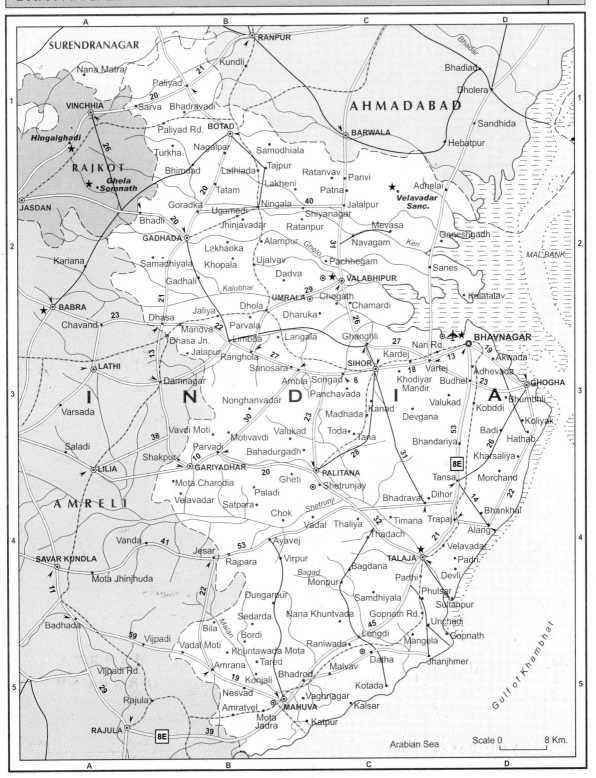

SURENDRANAGAR

Nana Matra
Paliyad
Kundli
RANPUR
21
Sarva
Bhadravadi
VINCHHIA
Hingalghadi
Turkha
Paliyad Rd.
BOTAD
26
Nagalpar
Samodhiala
RAJKOT
Bhimdad
Lathiada
Tajpur
Ratanvav
Panvi
Ghela Somnath
20
Tatam
Lakheni
Patna
Goradka
Ugamedi
Ningala
40
Jalalpur
JASDAN
Bhadi
20
Jhinjavadar
Shiyanagar
Adhelai
Velavadar Sanc.
GADHADA
Lakhanka
Ratanpur
Mevasa
Navagam
Keri
Ganeshgadh
Kariana
Samadhiyala
Khopala
Ujalvav
Alampur
31
Navagam
MAL BANK
Gadhali
Dadva
Pachhegam
Sanes
Kalubhar
Ghelo
VALABHIPUR
Kalatalav
21
Jaliya
Dhola
UMRALA
29
Chogath
Chamardi
BABRA
23
Dhasa
Parvala
Dharuka
Ghanghli
26
Nari Rd.
BHAVNAGAR
Chavand
22
Limbda
Langala
27
Kardej
13
Akwada
13
Mandva
Dhasa Jn.
Jalapur
Ranghola
27
Sanosara
SIHOR
18
Vartej
Adhevada
19
LATHI
Ambla
Songad
8
Khodiyar Mandir
Budhel
23
GHOGHA
Damnagar
Panchavada
Kanad
Valukad
Kobddi
Bhumbhli
Varsada
Nonghanvadar
30
Valukad
23
Madhada
Toda
Devgana
53
Badi
Koliyak
Saladi
Vavdi Moti
Motivavdi
Bahadurgadh
Tana
28
Bhandariya
Kharsaliya
Hathab
LILIA
38
Parvadi
10
Shakpur
GARIYADHAR
20
Gheti
PALITANA
8E
Tansa
Morchand
Mota Charodia
Paladi
Shetrunjay
Bhadraval
Dihor
14
22
Velavadar
Satpara
Chok
Shetrunji
Bhankhal
AMRELI
Vadal
Thaliya
32
Timana
Trapaj
21
Alang
Vanda
41
Jesar
53
Ayavej
Thadach
TALAJA
Velavadar
SAVAR KUNDLA
Rajpara
Virpur
Bagdana
Padri
Mota Jhinjhuda
11
Bagad
Monpur
Parthi
Devli
Phulsar
Badhada
22
Sedarda
Nana Khuntvada
Samdhiyala
Sultanpur
59
Vijpadi
Bila
Bordi
Gopnath Rd.
Unchadi
Gopnath
Vadal Moti
Malan
Raniwada
45
Longdi
Mangela
Vijpadi Rd.
Khuntawada Mota
Tared
Datha
Jhanjhmer
Amrana
Malvav
29
Rajula
19
Konjali
Bhadrod
Kotada
Nesvad
Vaghnagar
Kalsar
Amratvel
MAHUVA
Katpur
RAJULA
8E
39
Mota Jadra

INDIA

AHMADABAD

Bhadar
Bhadiad
Dholera
Sandhida
Hebatpur
BARWALA

Gulf of Khambhat

Arabian Sea

Scale 0   8 Km.

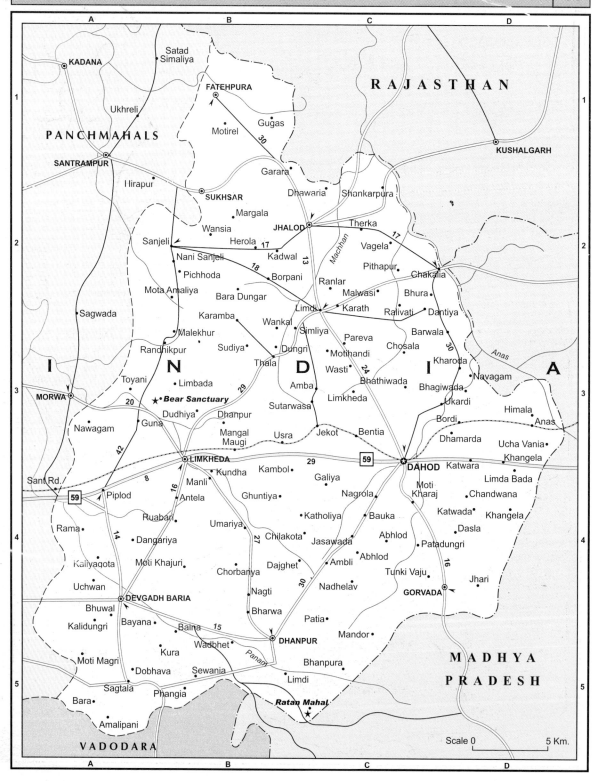

RAJASTHAN

PANCHMAHALS

KADANA

Satad
Simaliya

FATEHPURA

Ukhreli

Gugas

Motirel

KUSHALGARH

SANTRAMPUR

Hirapur

Garara

SUKHSAR

Dhawaria

Shankarpura

Margala

Wansia

Herola

Therka

JHALOD

Vagela

Sanjeli

17

Kadwal

Pithapur

Nani Sanjeli

18

13

Chakalia

Pichhoda

Borpani

Ranlar

Bhura

Mota Amaliya

Limdi

Malwasi

Dantiya

Karath

Ralivati

Sagwada

Bara Dungar

Karamba

Wankal

Simliya

Pareva

Chosala

Barwala

Malekhur

Sudiya

Dungri

Motihandi

Kharoda

Randhikpur

Thala

Wasti

Bhathiwada

Navagam

Toyani

Limbada

Amba

Limkheda

Bhagiwada

MORWA

20

29

★ Bear Sanctuary

Ukardi

Himala

Sutarwasa

Bordi

Anas

Nawagam

Dudhiya

Dhanpur

Usra

Jekot

Bentia

Dhamarda

Ucha Vania

Guna

42

Mangal
Maugi

Khangela

LIMKHEDA

29

59

DAHOD

Katwara

Limda Bada

8

Kundha

Kambol

Galiya

Moti
Kharaj

Chandwana

59

Manli

Ghuntiya

Nagrola

Katwada

Khangela

Piplod

Antela

Bauka

Dasla

Sant Rd.

16

Ruabari

Umariya

Katholiya

Abhlod

Patadungri

Rama

14

Dangariya

Chilakota

Jasawada

Abhlod

Moti Khajuri

27

Dajghet

Ambli

Tunki Vaju

Jhari

Kaliyaqota

Chorbanya

30

Nadhelav

GORVADA

Uchwan

DEVGADH BARIA

Nagti

Patia

Bhuwal

Bayana

Baina

Bharwa

Mandor

MADHYA

Kalidungri

15

PRADESH

Kura

Wadbhet

DHANPUR

Bhanpura

Moti Magri

Panam

Dobhava

Sewania

Limdi

Sagtala

Phangia

Bara

Ratan Mahal

★

Amalipani

VADODARA

Machhan

Anas

30

24

Scale 0   5 Km.

A   B   C   D

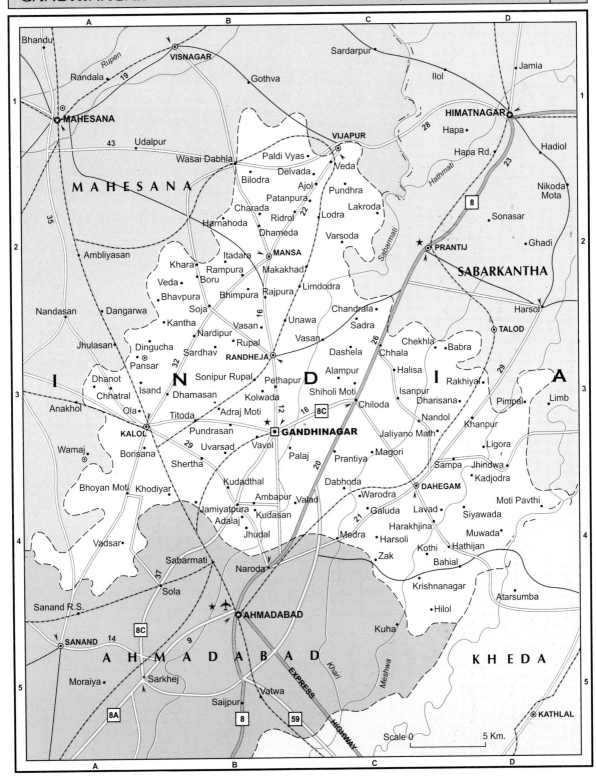

Map labels:

Bhandu, Rupen, VISNAGAR, Randala, 19, Gothva, Sardarpur, Ilol, Jamla, HIMATNAGAR, Hapa, Hapa Rd., Hadiol, MAHESANA, Udalpur, 43, Wasai Dabhla, Paldi Vyas, VIJAPUR, Veda, 28, Hathmati, 23, 8, Nikoda Mota, Delvada, Bilodra, Ajol, Pundhra, Sonasar, MAHESANA, Charada, Patanpura, Lakroda, Ghadi, Ridrol, Lodra, Harnahoda, Dhameda, Varsoda, Sabarmati, PRANTIJ, SABARKANTHA, Ambliyasan, Itadara, MANSA, Khara, Rampura, Makakhad, Harsol, Veda, Boru, Rajpura, Limdodra, 22, TALOD, Bhavpura, Bhimpura, Chandrala, Nandasan, Dangarwa, Soja, Unawa, Sadra, 29, Jhulasan, Kantha, Vasan, Vasan, Dashela, Chhala, Chekhla, Babra, A, Nardipur, Rupal, Halisa, Rakhiyal, Dingucha, Sardhav, RANDHEJA, Alampur, Isanpur, Pimpal, Limb, Dhanot, Pansar, 32, Sonipur Rupal, Pethapur, Shiholi Moti, Dharisana, Chhatral, Isand, Dhamasan, Kolwada, Chiloda, Nandol, Khanpur, Anakhol, Ola, Titoda, 12, 16, 8C, Jaliyano Math, Ligora, KALOL, Pundrasan, GANDHINAGAR, Magori, Jhindwa, Wamaj, 29, Uvarsad, Vavol, Palaj, Prantiya, Sampa, Kadjodra, Borisana, Shertha, 20, Dabhoda, DAHEGAM, Moti Pavthi, Bhoyan Moti, Khodiyar, Kudadthal, Warodra, Lavad, Siyawada, Ambapur, Valad, 21, Galuda, Harakhjina, Muwada, Jamiyatpura, Kudasan, Medra, Harsoli, Hathijan, Adalaj, Jhudal, Zak, Kothi, Bahial, Vadsar, Krishnanagar, Atarsumba, Sabarmati, 37, Naroda, Sola, Hilol, Kuha, KHEDA, Sanand R.S., AHMADABAD, 8C, SANAND, 14, 8C, 9, Khari, Meshwa, KATHLAL, Moraiya, Sarkhej, AHMADABAD, EXPRESS, 8A, Vatwa, Saijpur, 8, 59, HIGHWAY

Scale 0   5 Km.

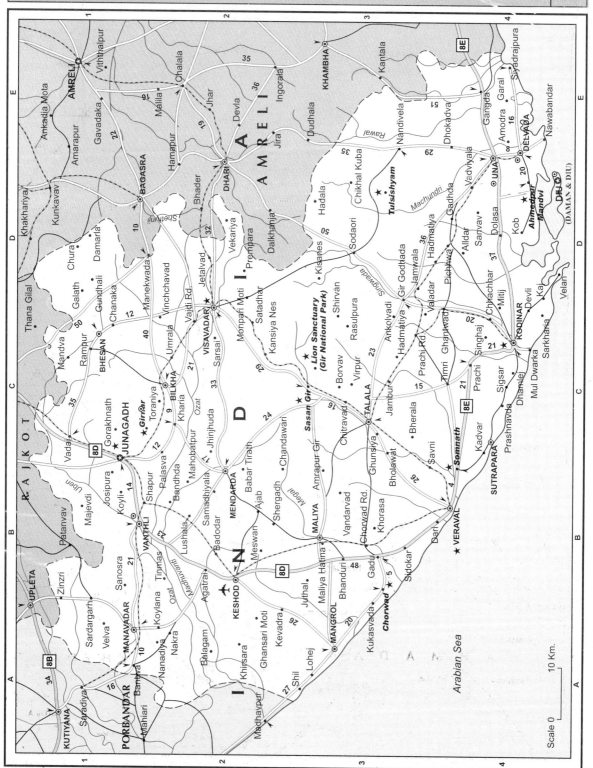

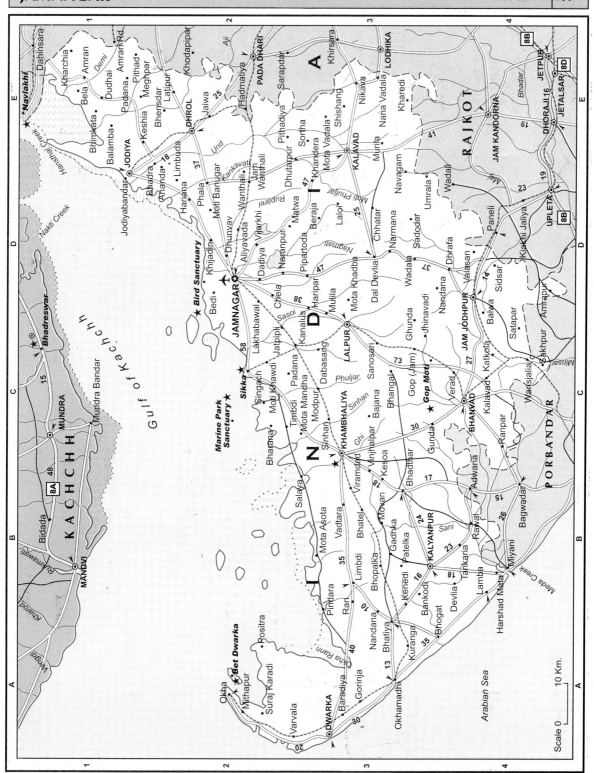

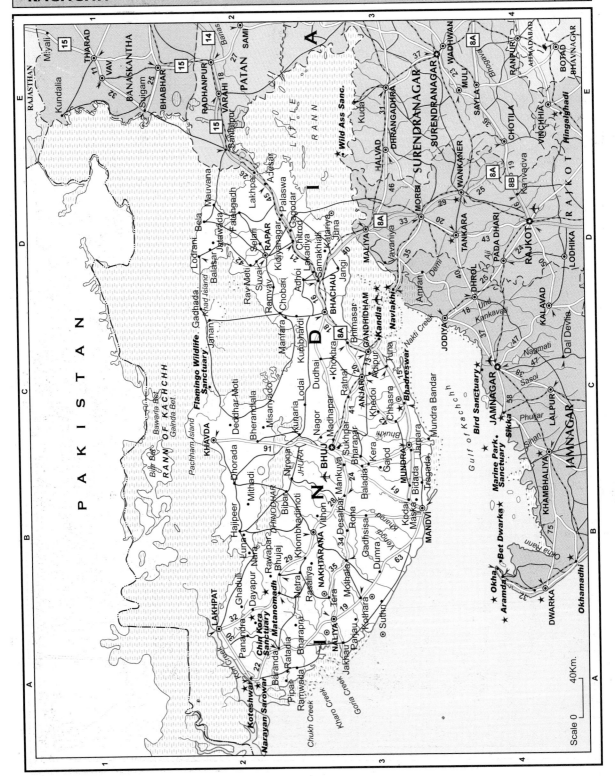

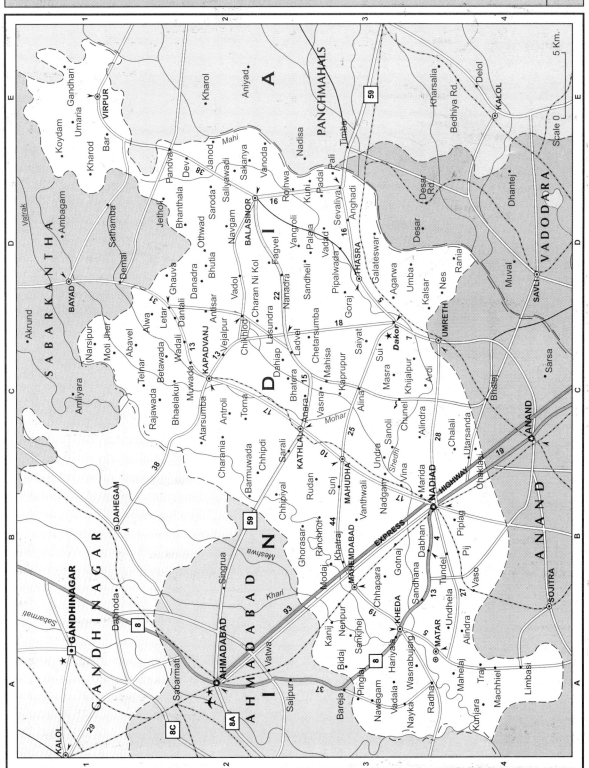

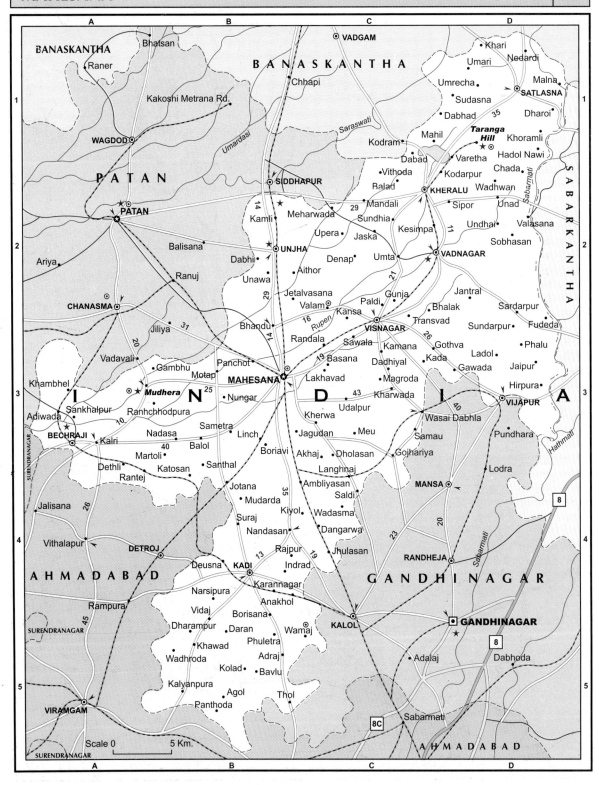

Scale 0   5 Km.

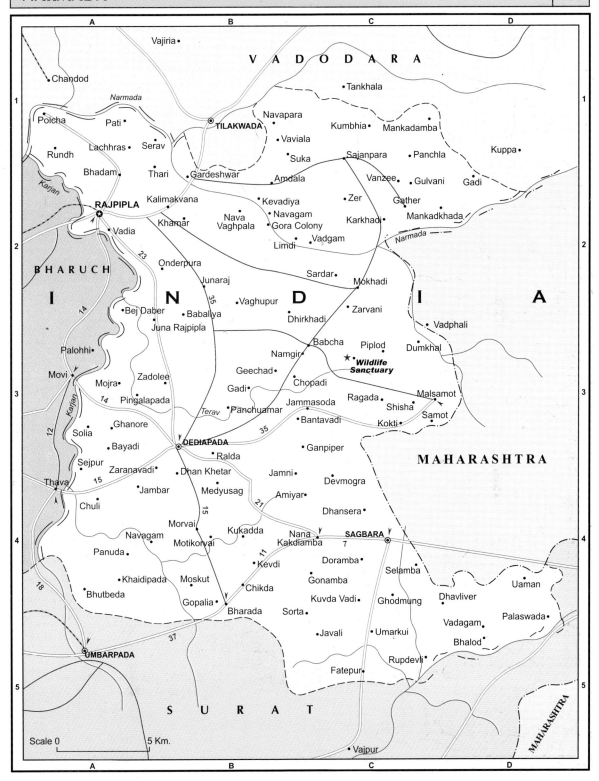

Scale 0   5 Km.

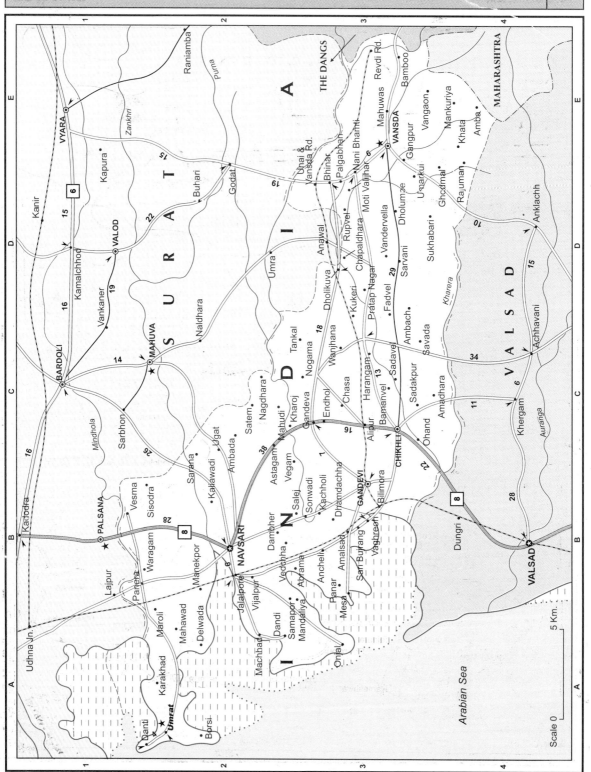

Map labels:

A · B · C · D

MODASA · 24

Malham · 18

DHANSURA · MALPUR

SABARKANTHA

BAKOR · Dilwas · Bachkariya · Godhar · RAJASTHAN

Vatrak · 14

BAYAD · Padedi · Munpur · Khedaya · Bureti

Gangta · Mahi · KADANA · Satad Simaliya

Vadagam · Hindoliya · Batakwada · FATEHPURA

Kanesar · Chitva · Dodiya · Ukhreli

Virpur · 40 · 29 · Malvan · SANTRAMPUR · 11 · 25 · Garara

Madhwas · Limra · Hirapur · 10 · SUKHSAR

Sathamba · Panapur · Anklava · Ghodhar · Gorhib · JHALOD

Undara · 30 · Padariya · Motisarsh · Limdi

Wardhari · Bhalada · LUNAVADA · Mulvan · Doli · 13 · Machhan

Pandav · Ravadia · Panam · Kanpur · Sarswa · Limbdi

Kharol · Kothamba · Boriya · Nasikpur · Sagwada · Rajayata

Dhamaniya · 19 · Bhadrala · 34 · Nada · Vandeli

BALASINOR · Mardeswar · Nandarva · 29

Dharapur · SHEHERA · MORWA · DAHOD

KHEDA · Vadi · Aniyad · Dalwada · Padard · 20

Nadisa · Rena · 21 · Mangliana · LIMKHEDA

Dhanitra · Bahi · Sampa · Chhavad · 18

Sevaliya · Kakanpur · Khandia · Sant Rd. · Piplod · 59

THASRA · 16 · Tuva · 5 · Tuwa · 15 · Kansudi · Chanthelav · 24 · Chilakota

Timba Rd. · Vavadi Khurd · GODHRA · 13 · 16

38 · Veganpur · Bhamaiya · Gollav

Desar · Mesri · Sansoli · Ambali · Kaliyakuva · DEVGADH BARIYA · 15 · DHANPUR

ANAND · Bedhiya Rd. · Kharsalia · Vejalpur · Simalia · Wadhhet · Panam

Pingli · 30 · Sureli · Sherpura · Vavkulli · Sagtala

Baksol · Delol · Adadara · GHOGAMBA · Ratan Mahal

KALOL · Vyasada · Kharod · MADHYA PRADESH

Champaner Rd. · 12 · Alwa · Raigadh · Zinzari · 53

SAVLI · 31 · Kanjari · Tarkhanda · Ranjitnagar · Deyhat

Karchiya · HALOL · 10 · Rayanwadiya · Nathpuja · Pani Mines · VADODARA

Pavagadh · Talavdi · Dungarwant · Sukhi

VADODARA · Jarod · Tajpura · Bamankuva

Shivraipur · Narukot · Dev

Kotambi · Rameshwar · JAMBUGHODA · JETPUR PAVI · Orsang · CHHOTA UDEPUR · MADHYA PRADESH

VAGHODIA · 41 · 37

VADODARA · Bodeli · Scale 0 — 5 Km.

I N D I A

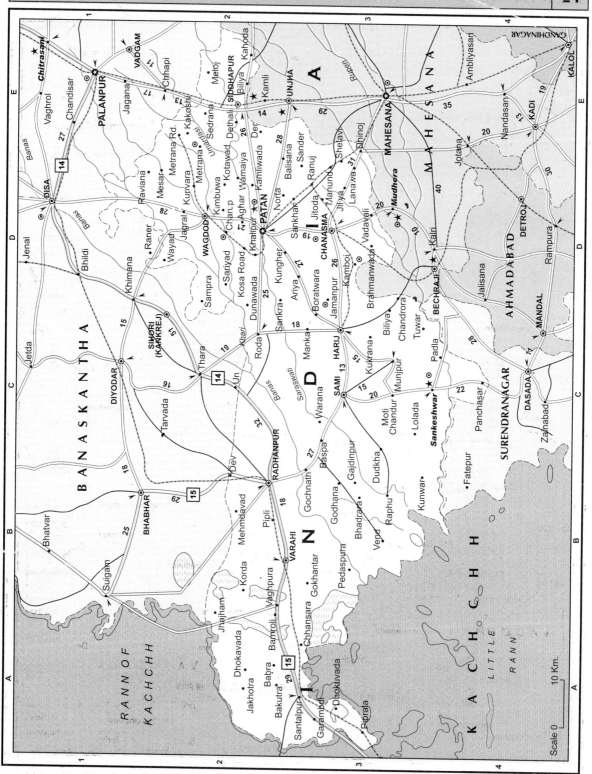

Scale 0   10 Km.

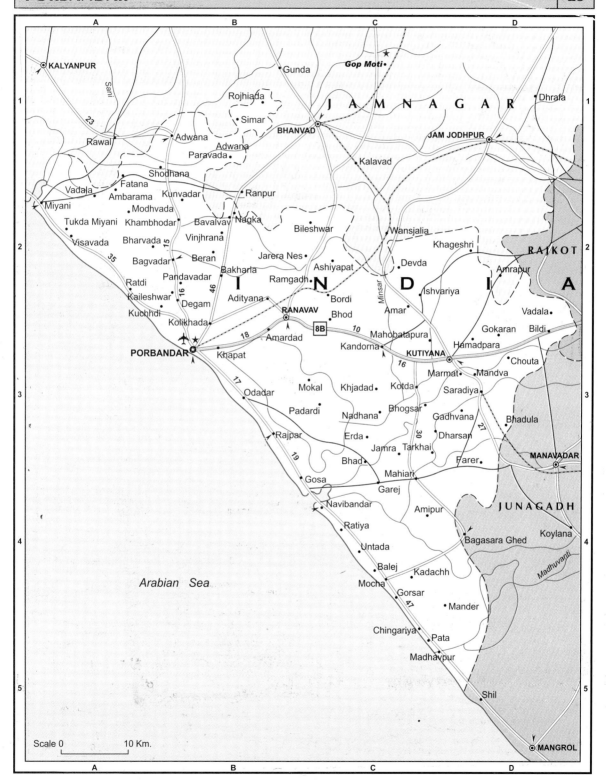

Scale 0   10 Km.

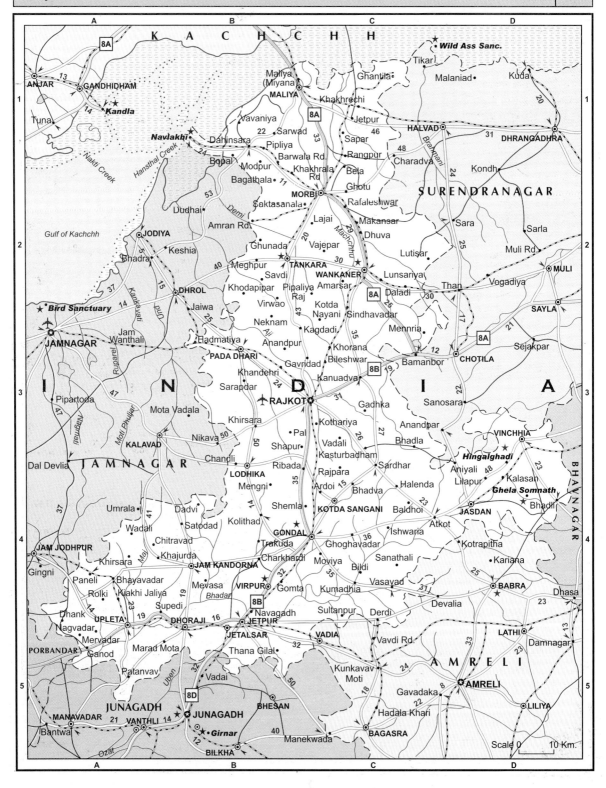

K A C H C H H

• Wild Ass Sanc.
Tikar ★

8A

ANJAR 13 GANDHIDHAM
14 ★ Kandla
Tuna

Maliya
(Miyana)
MALIYA
Khakhrechi
8A
Ghantila
Malaniad
Kuda
20
Jetpur
HALVAD
31 DHRANGADHRA

Navlakhi
Dahinsara 24
Bopal
Vavaniya 22 Sarwad 33
Pipliya
Barwala Rd.
Modpur
Bagathala 11
Khakhrala Rd.
Sapar 46
Rangpur
Charadva 48
Beta
Ghotu
MORBI
Saktasanala
Rafaleshwar
Makansar
Dhuva
SURENDRANAGAR
Sara
Sarla
Muli Rd.
MULI

Gulf of Kachchh
JODIYA
Bhadra
Keshia
53
Dudhai
Amran Rd.
Ghunada
Lajai
Vajepar
Meghpur
Savdi
TANKARA
WANKANER
Lunsariya
Lutisar
25
Than 30
Vogadiya
SAYLA

37
15
DHROL
Jaiwa
40
Khodapipar
Pipaliya
Raj
Amarsar
Kotda
Nayani
Sindhavadar
8A
Daladi
Mennria
8A
Sejakpar

★ Bird Sanctuary
Jam
Wanthli
JAMNAGAR
Hadmatiya
Neknam
Anandpur
Virwao
43
Kagdadi
35
Khorana
Bileshwar
Bamanbor
12
CHOTILA
17

I N D I A

Pipartoda
47
47
Mota Vadala
PADA DHARI
Khandehri
Sarapdar 24
Gavridad
RAJKOT
31
Kanuadva
8B 19
Gadhka
Sanosara
22

Khirsara
Nikava 50
KALAVAD
50
Shapur
Pal
Vadali
Kasturbadham
26 27
Bhadla
Anandpar
VINCHHIA
Chandli
LODHIKA
Ribada
Rajpara
Sardhar
Aniyali 48
Lilapur
Hingalghadi
Kalasan

JAMNAGAR
Dal Devlia
Mengni
35
Ardoi 15
Bhadva
Halenda
Ghela Somnath
Bhadli

37
Umrala 41
Dadvi
Satodad
Kolithad
Shemla
KOTDA SANGANI
Baldhoi
23
JASDAN
Atkot
Kotrapitha

Wadali
Chitravad
Khajurda
Mal
GONDAL
Trakuda
Ghoghavadar 36
Ishwaria
Kariana
25

JAM JODHPUR
Khirsara
Paneli
Charkhardi
Moviya
Sanathali
Vasayad 31
BABRA
Dhasa

Gingni
Rolki
Kiakhi Jaliya
Bhayavadar
Mevasa
Bhadar
VIRPUR
32
Gomta
35 Kumadhia
Bildi
Devalia
23

Dhank
Nagvadar
Mervadar
UPLETA 19
Supedi
19
DHORAJI 16
8B
Navagadh
JETPUR
Sultanpur
Derdi
33
LATHI
Damnagar
13
23

PORBANDAR
Ganod
Marad Mota
JETALSAR
Thana Gilal
VADIA
Vavdi Rd.
24
AMRELI
Patanvav
Uben
Vadai
32
BHESAN
Kunkavav
Moti
18
Gavadaka
8
AMRELI
LILIYA

JUNAGADH
8D
JUNAGADH
MANAVADAR 21 VANTHLI 14
★ Girnar
12
Manekwada
Hadala Khari
22
BAGASRA
Scale 0   10 Km.
Bantwa
Ozat
BILKHA

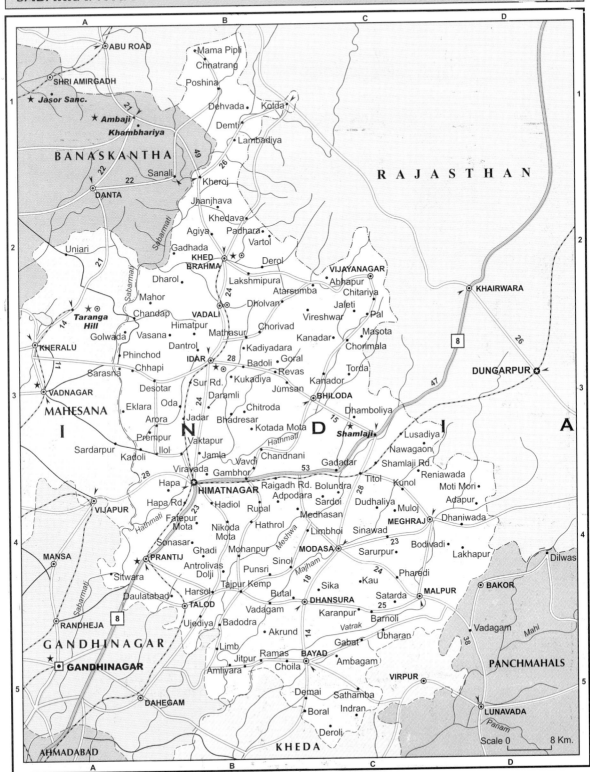

A B C D

ABU ROAD
Mama Pipli
Chnatrang
SHRI AMIRGADH
Poshina
★ Jasor Sanc.
1
Dehvada
Kotda
Demti
Ambaji
Khambhariya
Lambadiya

BANASKANTHA
Sanali
Kheroj
22
DANTA
Jhanjhava
Khedava
Uniari
Agiya
Padhara
2
Gadhada
Vartol
KHED
Derol
VIJAYANAGAR
BRAHMA
Abhapur
Dharol
Lakshmipura
Chitariya
KHAIRWARA
Mahor
Atarsumba
Jaleti
Pal
Chandap
VADALI
Dholvan
Vireshwar
Masota
Himatpur
Chorivad
Kanadar
Chorimala
8
Golwada
Mathasur
Vasana
Torda
DUNGARPUR
Phinchod
Dantrol
Kadiyadara
Goral
47
Chhapi
IDAR
28
Badoli
Revas
26
Sarasna
Sur Rd.
Kukadiya
Jümsan
Kanador
VADNAGAR
Desotar
Daramli
BHILODA
3
Eklara
Oda
Chitroda
Dhamboliya
MAHESANA
Arora
Jadar
Bhadresar
15
Prempur
Vaktapur
Kotada Mota
Shamlaji
Sardarpur
Ilol
Jamla
Chandnani
Lusadiya
Kadoli
Vavdi
Nawagaon
28
Viravada
Gambhor
53
Gadadar
Shamlaji Rd.
Hapa
Raigadh Rd. Bolundra
Titol
Reniawada
HIMATNAGAR
Kunol
Moti Mori
Hapa Rd.
Hadiol
Sardoi
Dudhaliya
Adapur
VIJAPUR
23
Rupal
Medhasan
Muloj
MEGHRAJ
Dhaniwada
Fatepur
Nikoda
Hathrol
Limbhoi
Sinawad
Mota
Mota
23
Bodivadi
4
MANSA
Sonasar
Ghadi
Mohanpur
MODASA
Sarurpur
Lakhapur
Dilwas
PRANTIJ
Antrolivas
Sinol
24
Pharedi
Sitwara
Dolji
Punsri
Sika
Kau
MALPUR
BAKOR
Daulatabad
Harsol
Tajpur Kemp
Satarda
25
Barnoli
Vadagam
RANDHEJA
8
Butal
DHANSURA
Karanpur
Ubharan
Vadagam
TALOD
Vadagam
38
GANDHINAGAR
Ujediya
Badodra
Akrund
14
Gabat
PANCHMAHALS
Limb
Ambagam
★
Jitpur
Ramas
BAYAD
GANDHINAGAR
Amliyara
Choila
VIRPUR
5
Demai
Sathamba
DAHEGAM
Boral
Indran
LUNAVADA
Deroli
Scale 0   8 Km.
AHMADABAD
KHEDA

A B C D

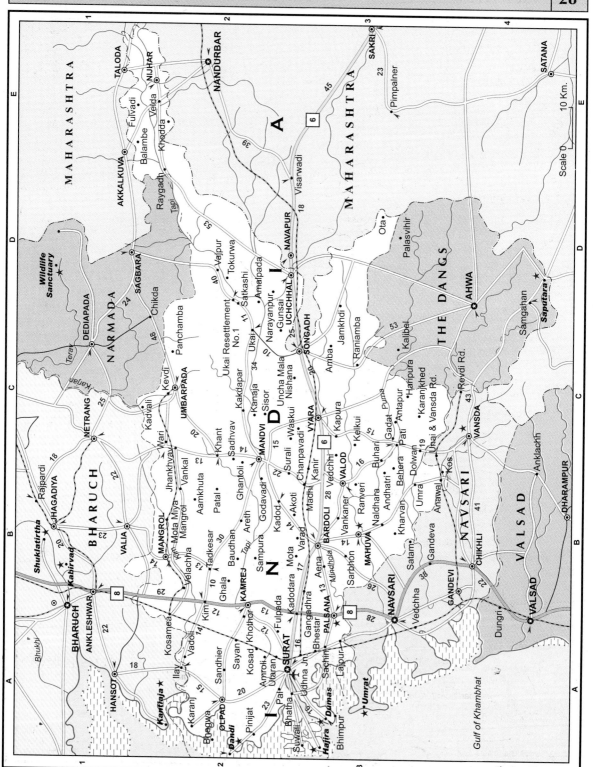

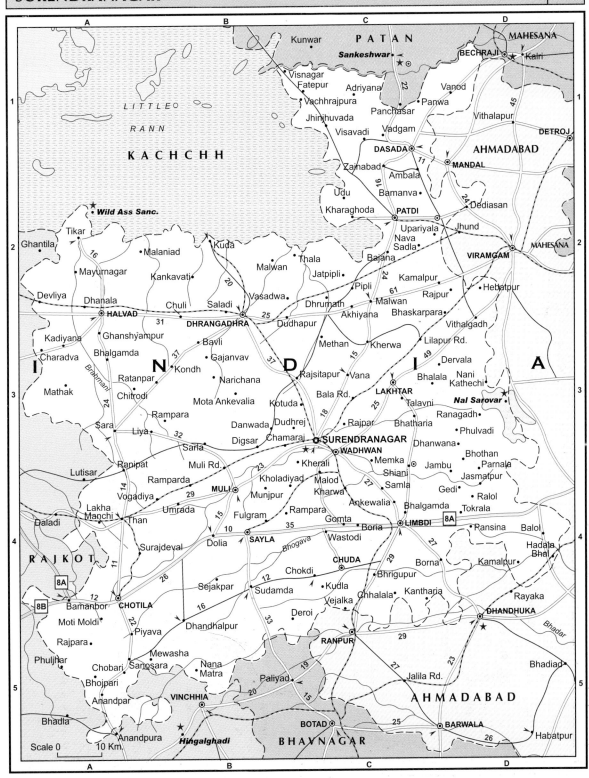

PATAN

Kunwar
Sankeshwar
MAHESANA
BECHRAJI
Kalri

Visnagar
Fatepur
Adriyana
Vanod
Panwa
Vachhrajpura
Panchasar
Vithalapur
Jhinjhuvada
Vadgam
DETROJ
Visavadi
DASADA
AHMADABAD
Zainabad
MANDAL
Ambala
Udu
Bamanva
Kharaghoda
PATDI
Dediasan
Upariyala
Jhund
Nava
Sadla
MAHESANA
Bajana
VIRAMGAM

LITTLE
RANN
KACHCHH

Wild Ass Sanc.
Tikar
Kuda
Thala
Kamalpur
Ghantila
Malaniad
Malwan
Jatpipli
Hebatpur
Mayurnagar
Kankavati
Pipli
Rajpur
Dhanala
Chuli
Saladi
Vasadwa
Dhrumath
Malwan
Bhaskarpara
Devliya
HALVAD
Akhiyana
Kadiyana
Ghanshyampur
DHRANGADHRA
Dudhapur
Vithalgadh
Charadva
Bhalgamda
Bavli
Methan
Kherwa
Lilapur Rd.
Mathak
Kondh
Gajanvav
Rajsitapur
Vana
Dervala
Ratanpar
Narichana
Bala Rd.
LAKHTAR
Bhalala
Nani
Chitrodi
Mota Ankevalia
Kotuda
Talavni
Kathechi
Rampara
Danwada
Dudhrej
Rajpar
Bhatharia
Nal Sarovar
Sara
Digsar
Chamaraj
SURENDRANAGAR
Ranagadh
Liya
Sarla
WADHWAN
Dhanwana
Phulvadi
Ranipat
Muli Rd.
Kherali
Memka
Jambu
Bhothan
Lutisar
Ramparda
Kholadiyad
Malod
Shiani
Parnala
Vogadiya
MULI
Munjpur
Kharwa
Samla
Jasmatpur
Lakha
Umrada
Fulgram
Ankewalia
Gedi
Ralol
Manchi
Than
Rampara
Bhalgamda
Tokrala
Daladi
Dolia
SAYLA
Gomta
Boria
LIMBDI
Ransina
Balol
Surajdeval
Wastodi
Hadala
Bhogava
CHUDA
Borna
Bhal
RAJKOT
Chokdi
Bhrigupur
Kamalpur
Sejakpar
Sudamda
Kudla
Rayaka
Bamanbor
CHOTILA
Chhalala
Kantharia
DHANDHUKA
Moti Moldi
Deroi
Vejalka
Bhadar
Rajpara
Piyava
Dhandhalpur
RANPUR
Jalila Rd.
Bhadiad
Phuljhar
Mewasha
Nana
Paliyad
Chobari
Sanosara
Matra
Bhojpari
BOTAD
BARWALA
Habatpur
Bhadla
Anandpur
VINCHHIA
AHMADABAD
Anandpura
Hingalghadi
BHAVNAGAR

Scale 0   10 Km.

8A   8B   8A

I N D I A
R A J K O T

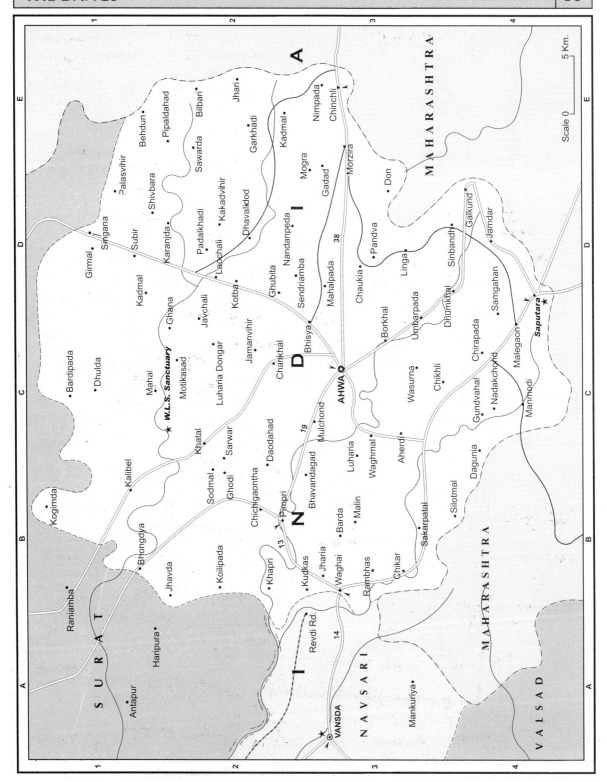

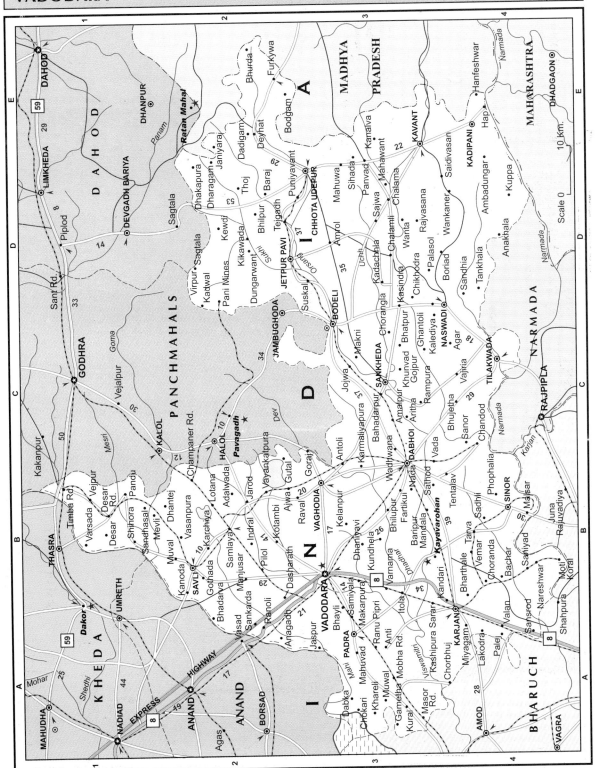

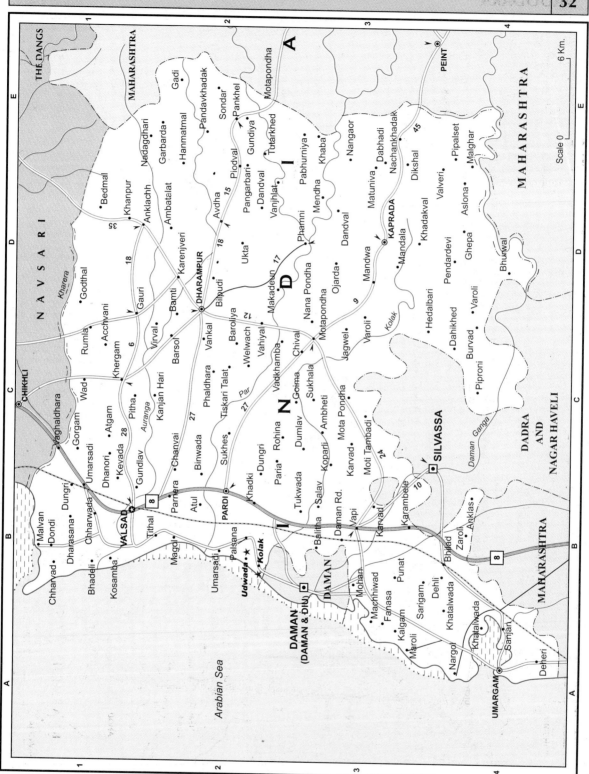

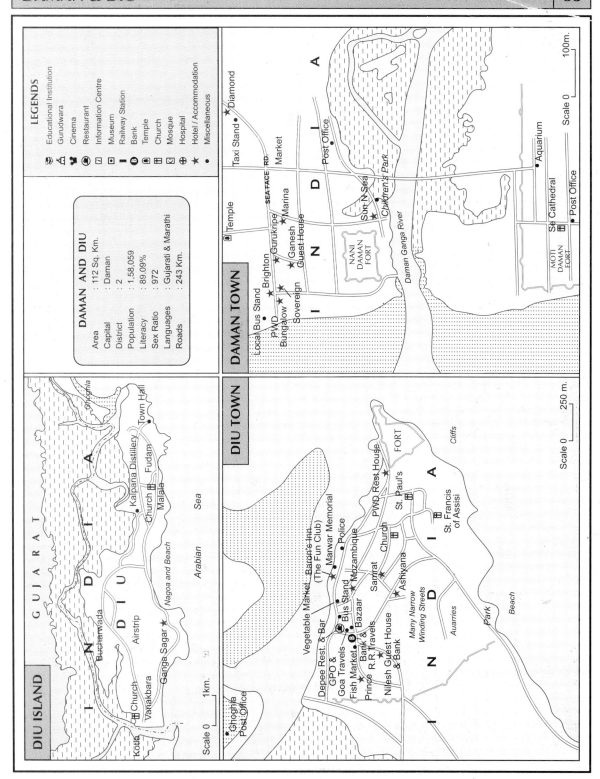

LEGENDS

	Educational Institution
	Gurudwara
	Cinema
	Restaurant
	Information Centre
	Museum
	Railway Station
	Bank
	Temple
	Church
	Mosque
	Hospital
	Hotel / Accommodation
	Miscellaneous

DAMAN AND DIU

Area	:	112 Sq. Km.
Capital	:	Daman
District	:	2
Population	:	1,58,059
Literacy	:	89.09%
Sex Ratio	:	972
Languages	:	Gujarati & Marathi
Roads	:	243 Km.

DAMAN TOWN

Taxi Stand • Diamond
Market
Post Office
SEA FACE RD.
Temple
Brighton
Gurukripe
Marina
Ganesh
Guest House
Sovereign
PWD
Bungalow
Local Bus Stand
Sun-N-Sea
Children's Park
Aquarium
Daman Ganga River
NANI DAMAN FORT
MOTI DAMAN FORT
St. Cathedral
Post Office
Scale 0 ___ 100 m.

DIU ISLAND

Ghoghla
Town Hall
Kalpana Distillery
Fudam
Church
Malala
Bucharwada
Airstrip
Ganga Sagar
Kotla
Vanakbara
Church
Nagoa and Beach
Arabian Sea
GUJARAT
INDIU
Ghoghla
Post Office
Scale 0 ___ 1 km.

DIU TOWN

FORT
Cliffs
PWD Rest House
St. Paul's
St. Francis of Assisi
Marwar Memorial
Baron's Inn (The Fun Club)
Police
Vegetable Market
Mozambique
Samrat
Church
Ashiyana
Bus Stand
Bazaar
Depee Rest. & Bar
GPO & Goa Travels
Fish Market
Bank &
Prince R.R. Travels
Nilesh Guest House & Bank
Many Narrow Winding Streets
Auarries
Park
Beach
INDIA
Scale 0 ___ 250 m.

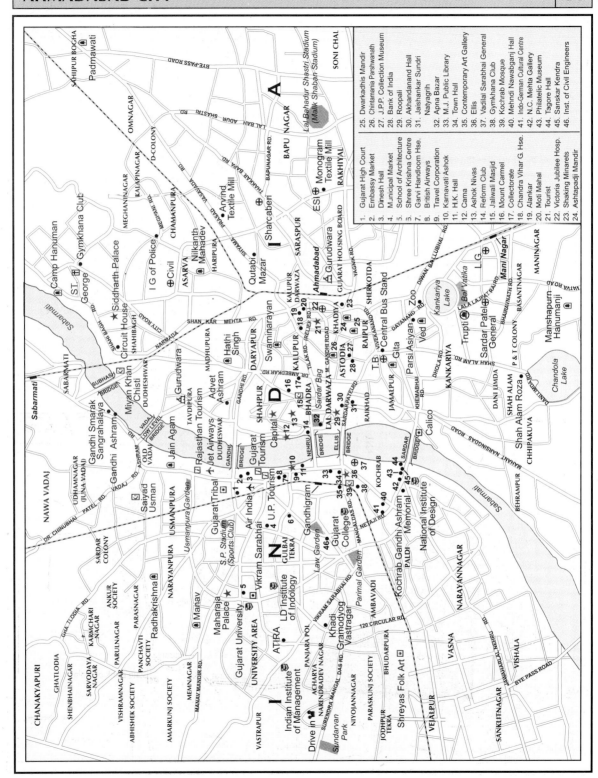

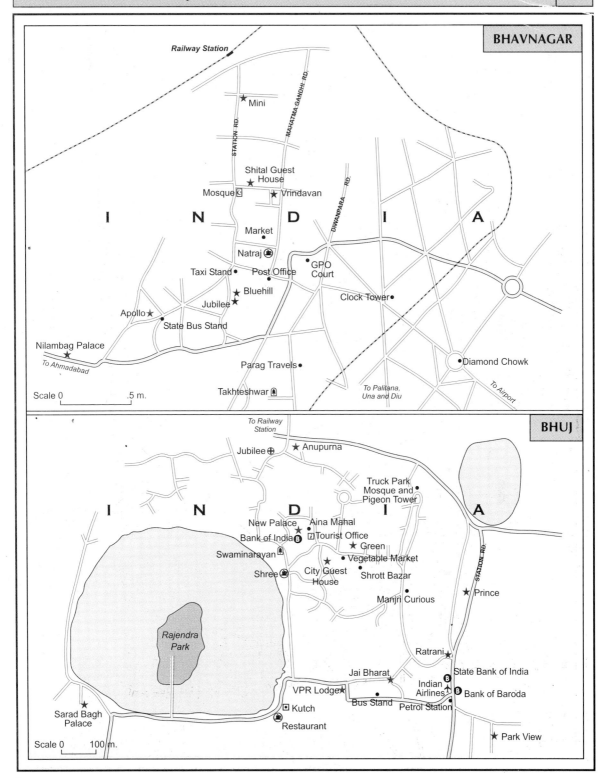

BHAVNAGAR

Railway Station

STATION RD.

MAHATMA GANDHI RD.

DIWANPARA RD.

★ Mini

Shital Guest House
★

Mosque ☪   ★ Vrindavan

I   N   D   I   A

Market

Natraj ⊛

Taxi Stand ●   Post Office ●   ● GPO
Court

★ Bluehill

Jubilee ★   Clock Tower ●

Apollo ★
●
State Bus Stand

Nilambag Palace
★
To Ahmadabad   Parag Travels ●

Scale 0 _____ .5 m.   Takhteshwar ▣   To Palitana, Una and Diu   Diamond Chowk ●   To Airport

---

BHUJ

To Railway Station

Jubilee ⊕   ★ Anupurna

Truck Park ●
Mosque and
Pigeon Tower

I   N   D   I   A

New Palace ★   Aina Mahal ★
Bank of India Ⓑ   ▣ Tourist Office
Swaminarayan ▥   ★ Green
Shree ⊛   ● Vegetable Market
City Guest   Shrott Bazar
House   Manjri Curious ●

STATION RD.

Rajendra
Park   ★ Prince

Ratrani ★

Jai Bharat   State Bank of India
★   Indian
VPR Lodge ★   Airlines Ⓑ   Ⓑ Bank of Baroda
Bus Stand   Petrol Station
Sarad Bagh   ● Kutch
Palace ★   ▣
Restaurant   ★ Park View

Scale 0 _____ 100 m.

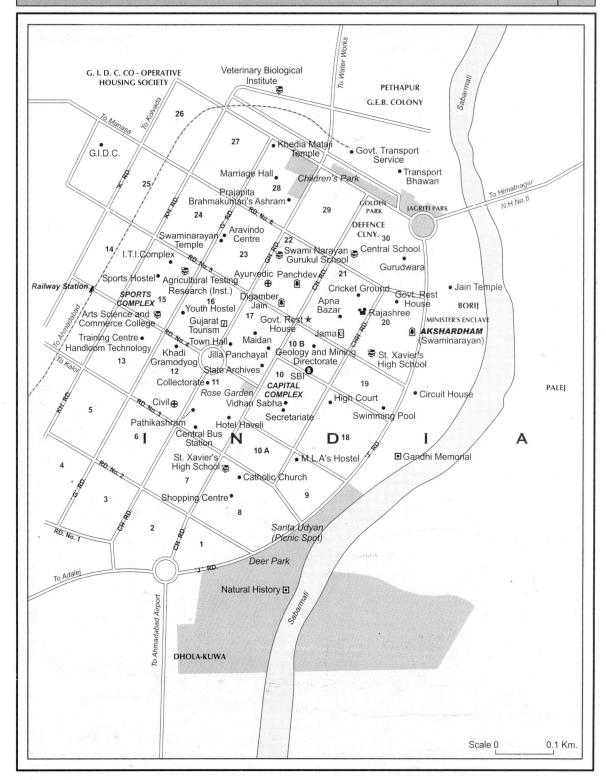

G. I. D. C. CO - OPERATIVE
HOUSING SOCIETY

Veterinary Biological
Institute

PETHAPUR
G.E.B. COLONY

To Manasa

To Kolvada

26

G.I.D.C.

25

27

Khedia Mataji
Temple

Govt. Transport
Service

Transport
Bhawan

To Himatnagar

N.H.No.8

Marriage Hall

Children's Park

28

GOLDEN
PARK

JAGRITI PARK

Prajapita
Brahmakumari's Ashram

29

DEFENCE
CLNY. 30

24

Swaminarayan
Temple

Aravindo
Centre

22

Swami Narayan
Gurukul School

Central School

Gurudwara

14

I.T.I.Complex

23

Ayurvedic Panchdev

21

Jain Temple

Sports Hostel

Agricultural Testing
Research (Inst.)

Digamber
Jain

Cricket Ground

Govt. Rest
House

BORIJ

Railway Station

SPORTS
COMPLEX 15

16

Youth Hostel

17

Apna
Bazar

Rajashree

20

MINISTER'S ENCLAVE

Arts Science and
Commerce College

Gujarat
Tourism

Govt. Rest
House

Jama

AKSHARDHAM
(Swaminarayan)

Training Centre
Handloom Technology

Town Hall

Maidan

10 B

Geology and Mining
Directorate

St. Xavier's
High School

13

Khadi
Gramodyog

12

Jilla Panchayat

State Archives

10

SBI

19

PALEJ

Collectorate 11

Rose Garden

CAPITAL
COMPLEX

High Court

Circuit House

5

Civil

Vidhan Sabha

Secretariate

Swimming Pool

Pathikashram

6

Hotel Haveli

I   N   D 18 I   A

Central Bus
Station

10 A

M.L.A's Hostel

Gandhi Memorial

4

St. Xavier's
High School

7

Catholic Church

9

3

2

Shopping Centre

8

RD. No. 1

1

Sarita Udyan
(Picnic Spot)

To Adalej

J. RD.

Deer Park

To Ahmadabad Airport

Natural History

DHOLA-KUWA

Sabarmati

Scale 0   0.1 Km.

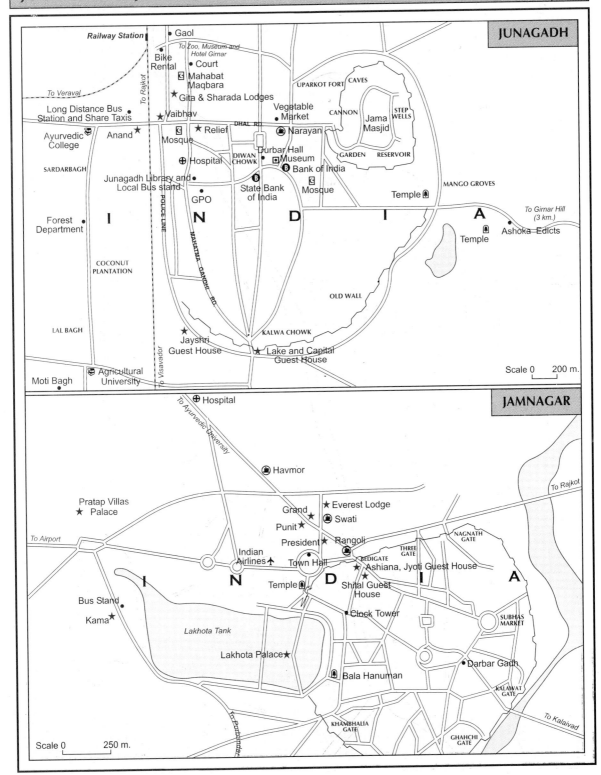

JUNAGADH

Railway Station
Gaol
Bike Rental
To Zoo, Museum and Hotel Girnar
Court
Mahabat Maqbara
Gita & Sharada Lodges
Vegetable Market
To Veraval
Long Distance Bus Station and Share Taxis
Vaibhav
DHAL RD.
UPARKOT FORT   CAVES
CANNON
Jama Masjid
STEP WELLS
To Rajkot
Ayurvedic College
Anand
Mosque
Relief
Narayan
Durbar Hall
Museum
Diwan Chowk
SARDARBAGH
Hospital
Bank of India
GARDEN   RESERVOIR
Junagadh Library and Local Bus stand
State Bank of India
Mosque
GPO
Temple
MANGO GROVES
To Girnar Hill (3 km.)
Forest Department
Ashoka Edicts
Temple
COCONUT PLANTATION
OLD WALL
LAL BAGH
Jayshri Guest House
KALWA CHOWK
Lake and Capital Guest House
Scale 0   200 m.
Moti Bagh
Agricultural University

I N D I A

JAMNAGAR

Hospital
To Ayurvedic University
Havmor
Pratap Villas Palace
Everest Lodge
Grand
Swati
Punit
President
Rangoli
To Rajkot
NAGNATH GATE
THREE GATE
BEDIGATE
To Airport
Indian Airlines
Town Hall
Ashiana, Jyoti Guest House
Temple
Shital Guest House
Bus Stand
Kama
Lakhota Tank
Clock Tower
SUBHAS MARKET
Lakhota Palace
Darbar Gadh
KALAWAT GATE
Bala Hanuman
To Kalaivad
KHAMBHALIA GATE
GHAHCHI GATE
Scale 0   250 m.

I N D I A

To Visavadar

To Porbandar

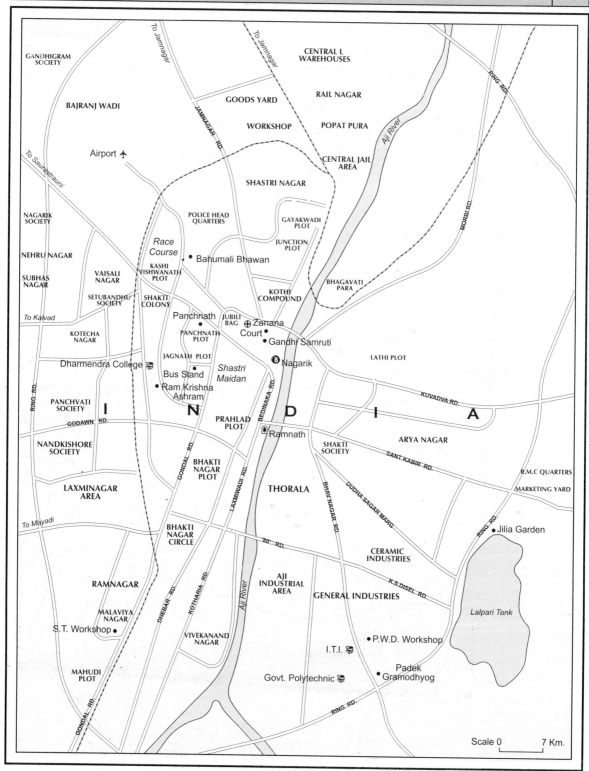

GANDHIGRAM SOCIETY

To Jamnagar

To Jamnagar

CENTRAL L WAREHOUSES

BAJRANJ WADI

GOODS YARD

RAIL NAGAR

WORKSHOP

POPAT PURA

JAMNAGAR RD.

Airport ✈

To Saurastrauni

CENTRAL JAIL AREA

SHASTRI NAGAR

Aji River

MORBI RD.

RING RD.

NAGARIK SOCIETY

POLICE HEAD QUARTERS

GAYAKWADI PLOT

NEHRU NAGAR

Race Course

• Bahumali Bhawan

JUNCTION PLOT

SUBHAS NAGAR

VAISALI NAGAR

KASHI VISHWANATH PLOT

KOTHI COMPOUND

BHAGAVATI PARA

To Kalvad

SETUBANDHU SOCIETY

SHAKTI COLONY

Panchnath •

JUBILI BAG

⊕ Zanana Court •

• Gandhi Samruti

LATHI PLOT

KOTECHA NAGAR

PANCHNATH PLOT

Ⓑ Nagarik

Dharmendra College 📖

JAGNATH PLOT

Bus Stand •

Shastri Maidan

I **N** **D** **I** **A**

• Ram Krishna Ashram

PANCHVATI SOCIETY

RING RD.

GODAWN RD.

PRAHLAD PLOT

⌂ Ramnath

KUVADVA RD.

SHAKTI SOCIETY

ARYA NAGAR

SANT KABIR RD.

NANDKISHORE SOCIETY

BEDINAKA RD.

BHAKTI NAGAR PLOT

GONDAL RD.

R.M.C QUARTERS

MARKETING YARD

To Mayadi

LAXMINAGAR AREA

LAXMINWADI RD.

BHAKTI NAGAR CIRCLE

THORALA

'80' RD.

BHAV NAGAR RD.

DUDHA SAGAR MARG

RING RD.

• Jilia Garden

RAMNAGAR

DHEBAR RD.

KOTHARIA RD.

Aji River

AJI INDUSTRIAL AREA

CERAMIC INDUSTRIES

K.S.DISEL RD.

Lalpari Tank

MALAVIYA NAGAR

GENERAL INDUSTRIES

S.T. Workshop •

VIVEKANAND NAGAR

• P.W.D. Workshop

MAHUDI PLOT

GONDAL RD.

I.T.I. 📖

Govt. Polytechnic 📖

• Padek Gramodhyog

RING RD.

Scale 0　　　　7 Km.

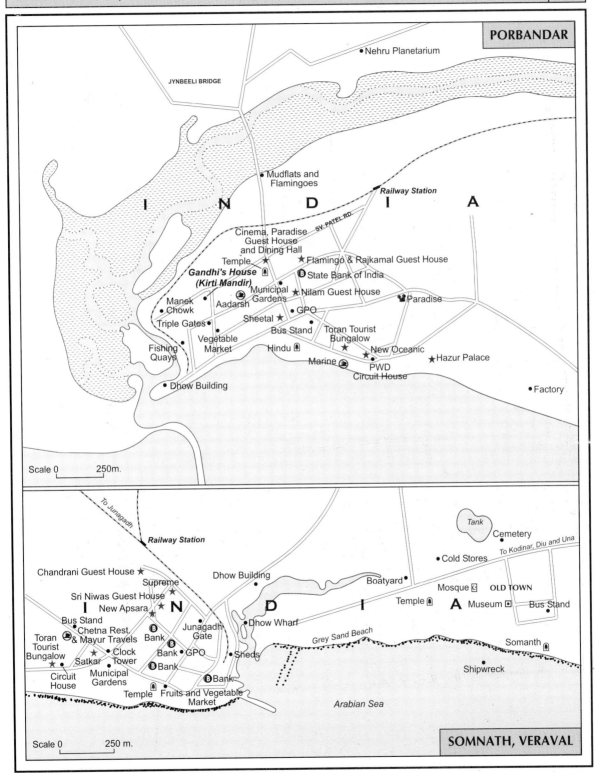

PORBANDAR

• Nehru Planetarium

JYNBEELI BRIDGE

I N D I A

• Mudflats and
Flamingoes

► *Railway Station*

SV. PATEL RD.

Cinema, Paradise
Guest House
and Dining Hall

Temple ★ ★Flamingo & Rajkamal Guest House

Gandhi's House Ⓑ State Bank of India
(Kirti Mandir)

Municipal ★ Nilam Guest House
Manek Gardens
• Chowk Aadarsh ★ Paradise
Triple Gates Sheetal ★ GPO

Vegetable Bus Stand Toran Tourist
Market Bungalow
Fishing Hindu ★ New Oceanic
Quays ★ ★ Hazur Palace
Marine PWD
• Dhow Building Circuit House

• Factory

Scale 0 ___ 250m.

I N D I A

To Junagadh

Railway Station

Tank
Cemetery •
Cold Stores *To Kodinar, Diu and Una*
Chandrani Guest House ★ Dhow Building •
Supreme Boatyard •
Sri Niwas Guest House ★ Mosque Ⓒ OLD TOWN
New Apsara ★ I N Temple D I A ⊡ Museum Bus Stand
Bus Stand
Toran Chetna Rest. Ⓑ Junagadh
Tourist & Mayur Travels Gate • Dhow Wharf Grey Sand Beach
Bungalow Bank Somanth
Bank Ⓑ GPO • Sheds
★ Satkar Clock • Shipwreck
Circuit Tower Ⓑ Bank
House Municipal
Gardens Ⓑ Bank
Temple Fruits and Vegetable *Arabian Sea*
Market

Scale 0 ___ 250 m.

SOMNATH, VERAVAL

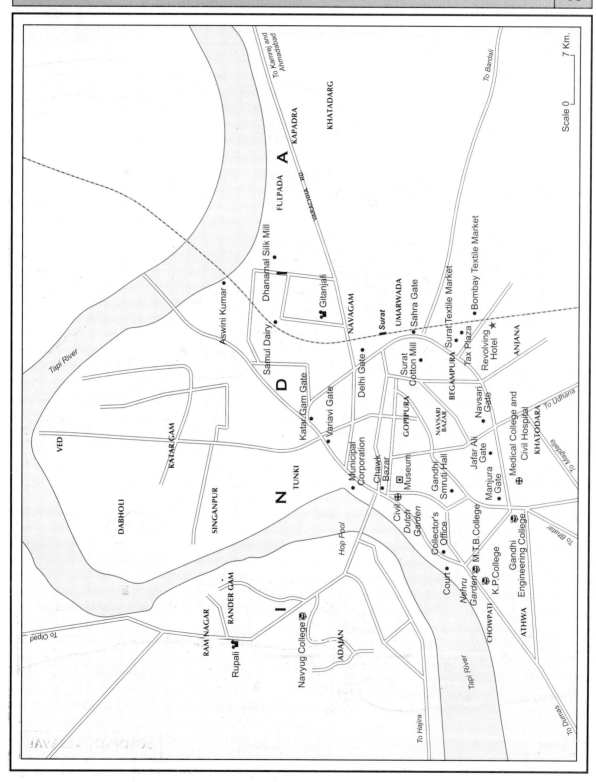

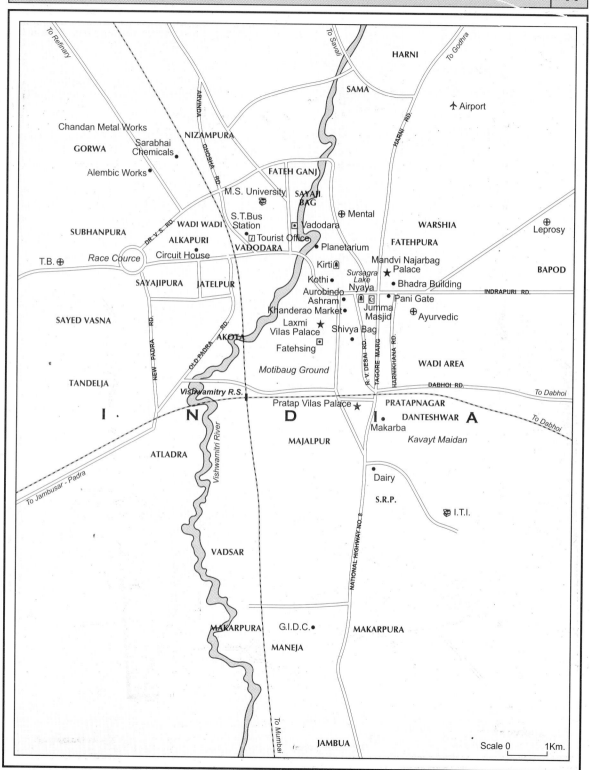

To Refinary
To Savali
To Godhra

HARNI

SAMA

Airport

Chandan Metal Works

NIZAMPURA

ARVINDA

GHOSHA RD.

HARNI RD.

GORWA
Sarabhai
Chemicals

Alembic Works

FATEH GANJ

M.S. University

SAYAJI
BAG

Mental

WARSHIA

Leprosy

SUBHANPURA

DR. Y.S. RD.

WADI WADI

S.T.Bus
Station

Vadodara

FATEHPURA

ALKAPURI

Tourist Office

VADODARA

Planetarium

T.B.

Race Cource

Circuit House

Kirti

Mandvi Najarbag
Palace

BAPOD

SAYAJIPURA

JATELPUR

Kothi

Sursagra
Lake

Nyaya

Bhadra Building

INDRAPURI RD.

SAYED VASNA

NEW PADRA RD.

OLD PADRA RD.

AKOTA

Aurobindo
Ashram

Khanderao Market

Laxmi
Vilas Palace

Fatehsing

Pani Gate

Jumma
Masjid

Ayurvedic

Shivya Bag

R.V. DESAI RD.

TAGORE MARG

HARNIKHANA RD.

WADI AREA

TANDELJA

Vishwamitry R.S.

Motibaug Ground

DABHOI RD.

To Dabhoi

Pratap Vilas Palace

PRATAPNAGAR

I . N . D . I . A

DANTESHWAR

To Dabhoi

ATLADRA

Vishwmitri River

MAJALPUR

Makarba

Kavayt Maidan

Dairy

S.R.P.

I.T.I.

VADSAR

NATIONAL HIGHWAY NO. 8

MAKARPURA

G.I.D.C.

MAKARPURA

MANEJA

To Mumbai

JAMBUA

Scale 0   1Km.

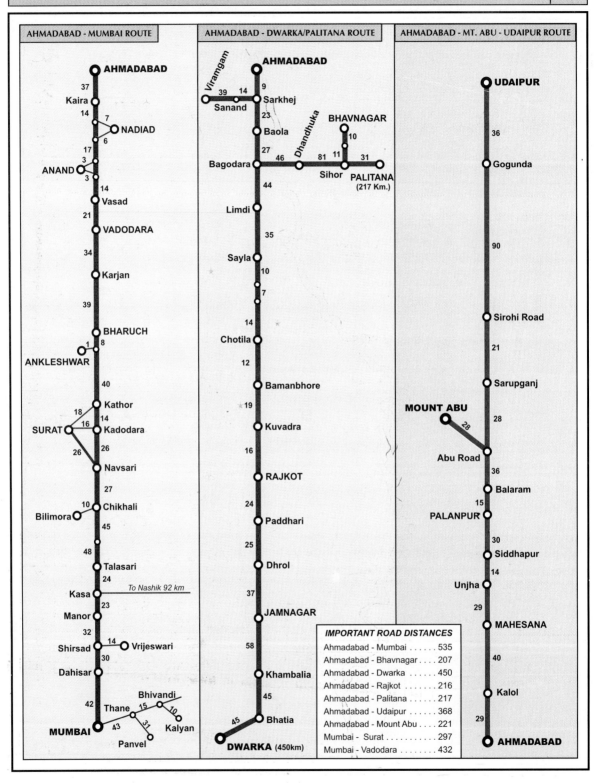

AHMADABAD - MUMBAI ROUTE

AHMADABAD
- 37
Kaira
- 14
- 7 NADIAD
- 6
- 17
- 3
ANAND
- 3
- 14
Vasad
- 21
VADODARA
- 34
Karjan
- 39
BHARUCH
- 1 — 8
ANKLESHWAR
- 40
Kathor
- 18 / 14
- 16
SURAT — Kadodara
- 26 / 26
Navsari
- 27
- 10 Chikhali
Bilimora
- 45
- 48
Talasari
- 24
Kasa   *To Nashik 92 km*
- 23
Manor
- 32
Shirsad — 14 — Vrijeswari
- 30
Dahisar
- 42   Bhivandi
Thane — 15 — 10
MUMBAI — 43 — 31 — Kalyan
Panvel

AHMADABAD - DWARKA/PALITANA ROUTE

AHMADABAD
Viramgam — 39 — 14 — 9 — Sarkhej
Sanand
- 23
Baola   BHAVNAGAR
- 27   Dhandhuka   10
Bagodara — 46 — 81 — 11 — 31 Sihor — PALITANA
- 44   Sihor   (217 Km.)
Limdi
- 35
Sayla
- 10
- 7
- 14
Chotila
- 12
Bamanbhore
- 19
Kuvadra
- 16
RAJKOT
- 24
Paddhari
- 25
Dhrol
- 37
JAMNAGAR
- 58
Khambalia
- 45
- 45 Bhatia
DWARKA (450km)

AHMADABAD - MT. ABU - UDAIPUR ROUTE

UDAIPUR
- 36
Gogunda
- 90
Sirohi Road
- 21
Sarupganj
MOUNT ABU
- 28
- 28
Abu Road
- 36
Balaram
- 15
PALANPUR
- 30
Siddhapur
- 14
Unjha
- 29
MAHESANA
- 40
Kalol
- 29
AHMADABAD

IMPORTANT ROAD DISTANCES	
Ahmadabad - Mumbai	535
Ahmadabad - Bhavnagar	207
Ahmadabad - Dwarka	450
Ahmadabad - Rajkot	216
Ahmadabad - Palitana	217
Ahmadabad - Udaipur	368
Ahmadabad - Mount Abu	221
Mumbai - Surat	297
Mumbai - Vadodara	432

AHMADABAD DISTRICT - Distance Chart

Distances in km.	AHMADABAD	AARNEJ	BAGODARA	BALWALA	BAVLA	DEHGAM	DHOLERA	DHOLKA	DHANDHUKA	LOTHAL	MANDAL	NAL SAROVAR	RANPUR	SANAND	SARANGPUR	VIRAMGAM
AHMADABAD	0	72	61	133	33	31	129	40	104	80	86	65	133	27	150	62
AARNEJ	72	0	11	65	39	103	61	40	36	5	95	41	60	57	139	71
BAGODARA	61	11	0	72	28	92	68	26	43	15	84	30	72	46	72	60
BALWALA	133	65	72	0	100	164	48	98	29	67	157	102	30	90	17	132
BAVLA	33	39	28	100	0	64	96	13	71	42	78	35	100	18	100	53
DEHGAM	31	103	92	164	64	0	160	71	135	111	117	96	104	58	181	93
DHOLERA	129	61	68	48	96	160	0	65	25	63	152	98	54	114	65	128
DHOLKA	40	40	26	98	13	71	65	0	69	30	91	56	98	31	115	68
DHANDHUKA	104	36	43	29	71	135	25	69	0	38	127	73	29	89	46	103
LOTHAL	80	5	15	67	42	111	63	30	38	0	100	45	67	60	89	75
MANDAL	86	95	84	157	78	117	152	91	127	100	0	55	156	60	174	25
NAL SAROVAR	65	41	30	102	35	96	98	56	73	45	55	0	102	38	102	30
RANPUR	133	60	72	30	100	164	54	98	29	67	156	102	0	118	30	32
SANAND	27	57	46	90	18	58	114	31	89	60	60	38	118	0	118	35
SARANGPUR	150	139	72	17	100	181	65	115	46	84	174	102	30	118	0	149
VIRAMGAM	62	71	60	132	53	93	128	68	103	75	25	30	132	35	149	0

AMRELI DISTRICT - Distance Chart

Distances in km.	AMRELI	BABRA	BAGASARA	CHALALA	CHITTAL	DAMNAGAR	DHARI	JAFRABAD	KHAMBHA	KODINAR	KUNKAVAV	LATHI	LILIA	RAJULA	VADLA	VICTOR
AMRELI	0	30	30	24	17	38	43	112	43	120	24	25	18	102	49	116
BABRA	30	0	60	54	11	42	73	128	89	166	54	21	44	104	75	120
BAGASARA	30	60	0	16	47	68	20	101	58	97	18	55	48	97	31	113
CHALALA	24	54	16	0	39	60	19	88	35	96	41	49	42	57	48	139
CHITTAL	17	11	47	39	0	43	58	137	74	135	41	30	35	117	66	131
DAMNAGAR	38	42	68	60	43	0	79	148	95	156	62	13	28	138	87	152
DHARI	43	73	20	19	58	79	0	91	38	77	40	60	53	69	46	85
JAFRABAD	112	128	101	88	137	148	91	0	53	85	114	123	116	24	124	40
KHAMBHA	43	89	58	35	74	95	38	53	0	105	81	84	77	32	106	48
KODINAR	120	166	97	96	135	156	77	85	105	0	115	145	138	95	124	111
KUNKAVAV	24	54	18	41	41	62	40	114	81	115	0	49	42	98	21	114
LATHI	25	21	55	49	30	13	60	123	84	145	49	0	120	127	70	136
LILIA	18	44	48	42	35	28	53	116	77	138	42	120	0	120	63	129
RAJULA	102	104	97	57	117	138	69	24	32	95	98	127	120	0	123	116
VADLA	49	75	31	48	56	87	46	124	106	124	21	70	63	123	0	112
VICTOR	116	120	113	139	131	152	85	40	48	111	114	136	129	16	112	0

BANASKANTHA DISTRICT - Distance Chart

Distances in km.	AMBAJI	BALARAM	BHABHAR	DANTA	DANTIWADA	DEESA	DIYODAR	DHANERA	PALANPUR	RADHANPUR	SANTALPUR	SHIHORI	THARAD	VADGAM	VARAHI	VAV
AMBAJI	0	45	141	22	90	85	123	115	60	158	208	114	141	75	161	154
BALARAM	45	0	96	53	45	40	78	70	15	113	163	69	96	30	138	109
BHABHAR	141	96	0	119	83	56	18	84	81	29	79	32	40	96	54	53
DANTA	22	53	119	0	68	63	101	93	38	136	186	92	119	53	161	132
DANTIWADA	90	45	83	68	0	27	65	57	30	100	150	56	83	45	125	96
DEESA	85	40	56	63	27	0	38	30	25	73	123	29	56	40	98	69
DIYODAR	123	78	18	101	65	38	0	74	63	35	85	18	42	78	60	55
DHANERA	115	71	84	93	57	30	74	0	55	109	159	59	44	70	134	57
PALANPUR	60	15	81	38	30	25	63	55	0	112	162	70	85	15	137	98
RADHANPUR	158	113	29	136	100	73	35	109	112	0	50	44	69	113	25	82
SANTALPUR	208	163	79	186	150	123	85	159	162	50	0	94	116	163	25	92
SHIHORI	114	69	32	92	56	29	18	59	70	44	94	0	60	54	69	73
THARAD	141	96	40	119	83	56	42	44	85	69	119	60	0	96	94	13
VADGAM	75	30	96	53	45	40	78	70	15	113	163	54	96	0	138	109
VARAHI	161	138	54	161	125	98	60	134	137	25	25	69	94	138	0	67
VAV	154	109	53	132	96	69	55	57	98	82	92	73	13	109	67	0

BHARUCH & NARMADA DISTRICT - Distance Chart

Distances in km.	AMOD	ANKLESHWAR	BHARUCH	DAHEJ	DEDIAPADA	GARHUDE-SHWAR	HANSOT	JAMBUSAR	JHAGADIA	NAVAGAM	NETRUNG	RAJPIPLA	SAGBARA	SHUKLATIRTH	VAGRA	VALIA
AMOD	0	48	35	46	120	140	69	11	68	143	94	123	147	40	17	72
ANKLESHWAR	48	0	13	55	72	92	21	59	20	95	40	75	99	31	33	24
BHARUCH	35	13	0	42	85	105	34	46	33	108	59	88	112	18	20	37
DAHEJ	46	55	42	0	127	147	76	57	75	150	101	130	154	57	32	79
DEDIAPADA	120	72	85	127	0	40	93	131	56	45	26	35	27	103	105	48
GARUDESHWAR	140	92	105	147	40	0	113	151	72	14	56	17	67	123	125	61
HANSOT	69	21	34	76	93	113	0	80	41	116	67	96	120	52	54	45
JAMBUSAR	11	59	46	57	131	151	80	0	79	154	105	134	158	51	28	83
JHAGADIA	68	20	33	75	56	72	41	79	0	75	30	55	119	30	53	44
NAVAGAM	143	95	108	150	45	14	116	154	75	0	52	23	81	126	128	80
NETRUNG	94	40	59	101	26	56	67	105	30	52	0	39	53	59	79	22
RAJPIPLA	123	75	88	130	35	17	96	134	55	23	39	0	62	106	108	61
SAGBARA	147	99	112	154	27	67	120	158	119	81	53	62	0	130	132	75
SHUKLATIRTH	40	31	18	57	103	123	52	51	30	126	59	106	130	0	38	58
VAGRA	17	33	20	32	105	125	54	28	53	128	79	108	132	38	0	57
VALIA	72	24	37	79	48	61	45	83	44	80	22	61	75	58	57	0

BHAVNAGAR DISTRICT - Distance Chart

Distances in km.	ALANG	BHAVNAGAR	BOTAD	GADHADA	GARIADHAR	GHOGHA	GOPNATH	MAHUVA	PALITANA	SAVARKUNDLA	SIHOR	SONGADH	TALAJA	UMRALA	VALLABHIPUR	VELAVADAR
ALANG	0	50	141	137	84	30	57	68	54	138	68	90	22	99	77	87
BHAVNAGAR	50	0	85	75	87	19	89	100	55	130	25	42	54	49	38	37
BOTAD	141	85	0	27	80	104	170	134	130	132	73	65	119	62	51	48
GADHADA	137	75	27	0	53	104	143	107	103	96	60	38	115	61	50	75
GARIADHAR	84	87	80	53	0	109	90	54	30	43	60	40	62	51	62	103
GHOGHA	30	19	104	104	109	0	82	93	74	163	44	66	47	68	57	56
GOPNATH	57	89	170	143	90	82	0	36	67	106	81	105	35	124	95	126
MAHUVA	68	100	134	107	54	93	36	0	78	70	92	94	46	131	124	137
PALITANA	54	55	130	103	30	74	67	78	0	73	30	38	32	56	53	79
SAVARKUNDLA	138	130	123	96	43	163	106	70	73	0	103	83	105	94	105	147
SIHOR	68	25	73	60	60	44	81	92	30	103	0	68	31	28	26	55
SONGADH	90	62	65	38	40	66	105	94	38	83	68	0	57	44	33	62
TALAJA	22	54	119	115	62	47	35	46	32	105	31	57	0	86	78	103
UMRALA	99	49	62	61	51	68	124	131	56	94	28	44	86	0	8	33
VALLABHIPUR	77	38	51	50	62	57	95	124	53	105	26	39	78	8	0	25
VELAVADAR	87	37	48	75	103	56	126	137	79	147	55	62	103	33	25	0

JAMNAGAR DISTRICT - Distance Chart

Distances in km.	BHANVAD	DHROL	DWARKA	GOP MOTI	HARSIDHMATA	JAMNAGAR	JAMJODHPUR	JODIYA	KALAVAD	KALYANPUR	LALPUR	MITHAPUR	OKHA	KHAMBHALIA	SALAYA	SIKKA
BHANVAD	0	173	105	20	50	73	127	199	102	68	39	105	135	30	42	62
DHROL	173	0	171	95	156	40	100	20	54	138	74	191	201	96	108	68
DWARKA	105	171	0	115	65	131	132	177	179	59	145	20	30	75	87	107
GOP MOTI	20	95	115	0	70	55	47	101	78	88	23	206	216	50	62	83
HARSIDHMATA	50	156	65	70	0	116	77	162	122	18	89	85	95	60	72	92
JAMNAGAR	73	40	131	55	116	0	60	46	48	98	34	151	161	56	68	28
JAMJODHPUR	127	100	132	47	77	60	0	106	75	95	66	152	162	57	69	88
JODIYA	199	20	177	101	162	46	106	0	74	144	80	197	207	102	114	174
KALAVAD	102	54	179	78	122	48	75	74	0	146	82	199	209	104	116	76
KALYANPUR	68	138	59	88	18	98	95	144	146	0	107	103	147	42	54	74
LALPUR	39	74	145	23	89	34	66	80	82	107	0	185	195	40	102	62
MITHAPUR	105	191	20	206	85	151	152	197	199	103	185	0	10	95	107	127
OKHA	135	201	30	226	95	161	162	207	209	147	195	10	0	105	117	137
KHAMBHALIA	30	96	75	50	60	56	57	102	104	42	40	95	105	0	12	32
SALAYA	42	108	87	62	72	68	69	114	116	54	102	107	117	12	0	44
SIKKA	62	68	107	83	92	28	88	174	76	74	62	127	137	32	47	0

JUNAGADH & PORBANDAR DISTRICT - Distance Chart

Distances in km.	BHESAN	CHORWAD	JUNAGADH	KESHOD	KUTIANA	MALIA	MANGROL	MANAVADAR	PORBANDAR	SASANGIR	SOMNATH	TAALA	TULSISHYAM	UNA	VERAVAL	VISVADAR
BHESAN	0	139	35	92	103	113	117	71	148	65	110	85	105	135	106	30
CHORWAD	133	0	98	41	132	20	20	84	103	66	29	51	161	111	25	102
JUNAGADH	35	98	0	40	68	78	82	36	113	60	98	75	138	135	94	65
KESHOD	92	41	40	0	91	21	25	59	83	64	52	53	143	113	46	67
KUTIANA	103	132	68	91	0	112	116	32	47	128	143	114	206	204	139	133
MALIA	113	20	78	21	112	0	20	80	103	47	31	32	122	92	27	72
MANGROL	117	20	82	25	116	20	0	84	83	67	49	52	142	112	45	92
MANAVADAR	71	84	36	59	32	80	84	0	77	96	111	112	174	172	107	101
PORBANDAR	148	103	113	83	47	103	83	77	0	151	132	135	225	195	128	150
SASANGIR	65	66	60	64	128	47	67	96	151	0	45	15	105	95	41	35
SOMNATH	110	29	58	52	143	31	49	111	132	45	0	30	112	82	4	80
TAALA	85	51	75	53	114	32	52	112	135	15	30	0	90	60	26	50
TULSISHYAM	105	161	138	143	206	122	162	174	225	105	112	90	0	30	116	75
UNA	135	111	135	113	204	92	112	172	195	75	82	60	30	0	86	105
VERAVAL	106	25	94	46	130	27	45	107	128	41	4	26	116	86	0	76
VISVADAR	30	102	65	67	133	72	92	101	150	35	80	50	86	105	76	0

KACHCHH DISTRICT - Distance Chart

Distances in km.	ANJAR	BHACHAU	BHADRE-SHWAR	BHUJ	GANDHIDHAM	KANDLA	LAKHPAT	MANDVI	MATANO-MADH	MUNDRA	NAKHATRANA	NALIYA	NARAYAN-SAROVAR	PANANDHRO	RAPAR	SAMKHIYALI
ANJAR	0	42	53	46	19	33	191	116	135	53	97	141	193	181	99	57
BHACHAU	42	0	68	72	39	46	231	156	175	95	137	181	233	221	59	17
BHADRESHWAR	53	68	0	76	34	46	221	68	165	24	127	150	226	211	127	85
BHUJ	46	72	76	0	63	77	151	60	90	52	52	100	147	136	142	102
GANDHIDHAM	19	39	34	63	0	14	210	102	154	78	116	160	212	200	93	51
KANDLA	33	46	46	77	14	0	222	114	166	70	128	172	224	212	105	63
LAKHPAT	191	231	221	151	210	222	0	183	56	197	94	101	49	37	268	226
MANDVI	116	156	68	60	102	114	183	0	149	44	111	81	154	166	196	154
MATANO MADH	135	175	165	90	154	166	56	149	0	141	38	45	58	46	212	170
MUNDRA	53	95	24	52	78	70	197	44	141	0	103	126	199	187	151	109
NAKHATRANA	97	137	127	52	116	128	94	111	38	103	0	55	96	84	168	132
NALIYA	141	181	150	100	160	172	101	81	54	126	55	0	72	84	218	176
NARAYAN SAROVAR	193	233	226	147	212	224	49	154	58	199	96	72	0	12	270	228
PANANDHRO	181	221	211	136	200	212	37	166	46	187	84	84	12	0	258	216
RAPAR	99	59	127	142	93	105	268	169	212	151	168	218	270	258	0	42
SAMKHIYALI	57	17	85	102	51	63	226	154	170	109	132	176	228	216	42	0

KHEDA & ANAND DISTRICT - Distance Chart

Distances in km.	ANAND	BALASINOR	BORSAD	DAKOR	KAPADVANJ	KHEDA	KHAMBHAT	MAHUDHA	MAHEMDABAD	MATAR	NADIAD	PETLAD	SEVALIA	THASARA	UMARETH	DHUVARAN
ANAND	0	76	21	39	70	40	60	38	42	42	21	43	63	44	32	49
BALASINOR	76	0	97	37	34	84	136	50	66	88	67	101	16	32	44	104
BORSAD	21	97	0	60	89	62	39	68	63	56	51	22	81	65	53	28
DAKOR	39	37	60	0	91	54	99	22	38	56	35	64	23	5	7	88
KAPADVANJ	70	34	89	91	0	61	110	27	43	67	44	73	50	36	38	119
KHEDA	40	84	62	54	61	0	56	34	18	6	19	48	75	59	47	77
KHAMBHAT	60	136	39	99	110	56	0	83	74	50	66	37	122	106	94	21
MAHUDHA	38	50	68	22	27	34	83	0	16	38	17	46	43	27	29	111
MAHEMDABAD	42	66	63	38	43	18	74	16	0	24	21	50	59	43	45	91
MATAR	42	88	56	56	67	6	50	38	24	0	21	50	77	61	49	71
NADIAD	21	67	51	35	44	19	66	17	21	21	0	29	56	40	28	70
PETLAD	43	101	22	64	73	48	37	46	50	50	29	0	85	69	57	40
SEVALIA	63	16	81	23	50	75	122	43	59	77	56	85	0	16	28	100
THASARA	44	32	65	5	36	59	106	27	43	61	40	69	16	0	12	93
UMARETH	32	44	53	7	38	47	94	29	45	49	28	57	28	12	0	81
DHUVARAN	49	104	28	88	119	77	21	111	91	71	70	40	100	93	81	0

MAHESANA & PATAN DISTRICT - Distance Chart

Distances in km.	BECHARAJI	CHANASMA	KADI	KALOL	HARIJ	KHERALU	MAHUDI	MANSA	MAHESANA	MODHERA	PATAN	SAMI	SHAN-KHESHVAR	SIDHAPUR	TARANGA HILL	VIJAPUR
BECHARAJI	0	33	46	66	54	77	85	80	35	14	53	59	46	75	92	82
CHANASMA	33	0	74	78	21	73	83	78	33	19	18	36	51	44	89	88
KADI	46	74	0	18	94	82	66	41	49	60	92	97	72	79	98	63
KALOL	66	78	18	0	99	87	48	23	45	70	96	114	90	84	103	45
HARIJ	54	21	94	99	0	82	107	100	54	40	27	15	40	5	98	105
KHERALU	77	73	82	87	82	0	58	63	42	67	55	97	122	31	16	49
MAHUDI	85	83	66	48	107	58	0	25	53	98	104	122	138	92	74	9
MANSA	80	78	41	23	100	63	25	0	45	70	76	114	113	84	79	22
MAHESANA	35	33	49	45	54	42	53	45	0	25	51	69	94	39	56	50
MODHERA	14	19	60	70	40	67	78	70	25	0	37	55	80	65	83	75
PATAN	53	18	92	96	27	55	104	96	51	37	0	42	67	28	71	101
SAMI	59	36	97	114	15	97	122	114	69	55	42	0	25	70	113	119
SHANKHESHVAR	46	51	72	90	40	122	138	113	94	80	67	25	0	95	138	144
SIDHAPUR	75	44	79	84	55	31	92	84	39	65	28	70	95	0	45	89
TARANGA HILL	92	89	98	103	98	16	74	79	56	83	71	113	138	45	0	65
VIJAPUR	82	88	63	45	105	49	9	22	50	75	101	119	144	89	65	0

PANCHMAHALS & DAHOD DISTRICT - Distance Chart

Distances in km.	DEVGADH BARIA	DAHOD	GHALOD	GODHRA	HALOL	JAMBUGHODA	KADANA	KALOL	LIMDI	LIMKHEDA	LUNAVADA	PAVAGADH	PIPLOD	SANTRAMPUR	SHAHERA	VANAK BORI
DEVGADH BARIA	0	51	62	57	96	123	79	83	51	27	94	103	15	67	77	91
DAHOD	51	0	35	78	117	144	77	104	24	24	95	124	36	65	98	112
GHALOD	62	35	0	89	128	155	42	115	11	59	60	135	47	30	77	123
GODHRA	57	78	89	0	39	66	79	26	78	54	37	46	42	67	20	34
HALOL	96	117	128	39	0	27	118	13	117	93	76	7	81	106	59	73
JAMBUGHODA	123	144	155	66	27	0	145	40	144	125	103	20	107	133	86	100
KADANA	79	77	42	79	118	145	0	105	53	76	42	113	64	12	59	89
KALOL	83	104	115	26	13	40	105	0	104	85	63	20	68	93	46	60
LIMDI	51	24	11	78	117	144	53	104	0	48	71	124	36	41	88	112
LIMKHEDA	27	24	59	54	93	125	76	85	48	0	91	100	12	89	74	88
LUNAVADA	94	95	60	37	76	103	42	63	71	91	0	83	82	30	17	47
PAVAGADH	103	124	135	46	7	20	113	20	124	100	83	0	88	113	66	80
PIPLOD	15	36	47	42	81	107	64	68	36	12	82	88	0	52	62	76
SANTRAMPUR	67	65	30	67	106	133	12	93	41	89	30	113	52	0	47	77
SHAHERA	77	98	77	20	59	86	59	46	88	74	17	66	62	47	0	30
VANAK BORI	91	112	123	34	73	100	89	60	112	88	47	80	76	77	30	0

RAJKOT DISTRICT - Distance Chart

Distances in km.	DHORAJI	GONDAL	JAM KUNDORNA	JASDAN	JETPUR	KOTDA SANGANI	LODHIKA	MALIA	MORBI	NAVLAKHI	PADDHARI	RAJKOT	TANKARA	UPLETA	VIRPUR	WANKANER
DHORAJI	0	49	20	66	79	59	84	187	155	199	115	88	132	19	55	141
GONDAL	49	0	36	47	30	10	35	138	106	150	66	39	83	68	14	92
JAMKUNDORNA	20	36	0	83	39	46	71	173	141	185	101	74	118	39	50	128
JASDAN	66	47	83	0	77	47	82	158	126	170	86	59	103	115	61	172
JETPUR	19	30	39	77	0	40	65	168	136	180	96	69	113	38	17	122
KOTDA SANGANI	59	10	46	47	40	0	45	134	102	146	62	35	79	78	24	88
LODHIKA	84	35	71	82	65	45	0	133	101	145	61	34	78	103	49	87
MALIA	187	138	173	158	168	134	133	0	32	42	89	99	55	206	152	59
MORBI	155	106	141	128	136	102	101	32	0	44	57	67	23	174	120	27
NAVLAKHI	199	150	185	170	180	146	145	42	44	0	101	117	67	218	164	71
PADDHARI	115	66	101	86	96	62	61	89	57	101	0	27	34	134	80	80
RAJKOT	88	39	74	59	69	35	34	99	67	117	27	0	44	107	53	53
TANKARA	132	83	118	103	113	79	78	55	23	67	34	44	0	151	97	50
UPLETA	19	68	39	115	38	78	103	206	174	218	134	107	151	0	69	160
VIRPUR	55	14	50	61	17	24	49	152	120	164	80	53	97	69	0	106
WANKANER	141	92	128	112	122	88	87	59	27	71	89	53	50	160	106	0

SABARKANTHA DISTRICT - Distance Chart

	BAYAD	BHILODA	DHANSURA	HARSOL	HIMATNAGAR	IDAR	KHED BRAHMA	MALPUR	MEGHRAJ	MODASA	PRANTIJ	RAYGADH	SHAMLAJI	TALOD	VADALI	VIJAYNAGAR
BAYAD	0	79	76	46	78	107	134	41	55	32	59	51	60	46	119	115
BHILODA	79	0	63	67	43	28	55	64	66	47	64	28	15	67	40	36
DHANSURA	76	63	0	30	62	91	118	25	39	16	43	35	44	30	103	99
HARSOL	46	67	30	0	39	67	94	48	62	39	20	32	51	7	81	96
HIMATNAGAR	78	43	62	39	0	28	55	67	69	46	21	27	46	39	40	78
IDAR	107	28	91	67	28	0	27	96	98	75	49	55	43	67	12	38
KHED BRAHMA	134	55	118	94	55	27	0	123	125	102	76	82	70	94	15	65
MALPUR	41	64	25	48	67	96	123	0	20	21	68	40	51	55	108	104
MEGHRAJ	55	66	39	62	69	98	125	20	0	23	82	42	49	69	110	106
MODASA	32	47	16	39	46	75	102	21	23	0	59	19	28	46	87	83
PRANTIJ	59	64	43	20	21	49	76	68	82	59	0	48	67	18	61	99
RAYGADH	51	28	35	32	27	55	83	40	42	19	48	0	19	39	68	64
SHAMLAJI	60	15	44	51	46	43	70	51	49	28	67	19	0	58	55	51
TALOD	46	67	30	7	39	67	94	55	69	46	18	39	58	0	79	103
VADALI	119	40	103	81	40	12	15	108	110	87	61	68	55	79	0	50
VIJAYNAGAR	115	36	99	96	78	38	65	104	106	83	99	64	51	103	50	0
Distances in km.	BAYAD	BHILODA	DHANSURA	HARSOL	HIMATNAGAR	IDAR	KHED BRAHMA	MALPUR	MEGHRAJ	MODASA	PRANTIJ	RAYGADH	SHAMLAJI	TALOD	VADALI	VIJAYNAGAR

SURT & DANG DISTRICT - Distance Chart

	AHWA	BARDOLI	DUMAS	HAJIRA	KANKRAPAR	KAMREJ	MANDVI	MANGROL	NIJHAR	OLPAD	SAPUTARA	SURAT	UCHCHHAL	UKAI	VALOD	VYARA
AHWA	0	109	156	162	93	158	113	143	130	161	45	140	77	66	97	78
BARDOLI	109	0	47	53	36	30	26	65	129	52	129	31	73	51	19	31
DUMAS	156	47	0	22	83	34	73	67	176	37	176	16	120	98	66	78
HAJIRA	162	53	22	0	90	40	79	73	182	31	182	22	126	104	70	84
KANKRAPAR	93	36	83	90	0	50	10	30	91	88	121	67	38	15	34	15
KAMREJ	158	30	34	40	50	0	37	33	158	24	160	18	102	65	49	61
MANDVI	113	26	73	79	10	37	0	30	101	69	133	57	48	25	23	35
MANGROL	143	65	67	73	30	33	30	0	125	50	166	31	72	55	52	65
NIJHAR	130	129	176	182	91	158	101	125	0	181	175	160	53	88	113	95
OLPAD	161	52	37	31	88	24	69	50	181	0	181	21	125	103	71	83
SAPUTARA	45	129	176	182	121	160	133	166	175	181	0	160	122	111	113	106
SURAT	140	31	16	22	67	18	57	31	160	21	160	0	104	67	34	62
UCHCHHAL	77	73	120	126	38	102	48	72	125	125	122	104	0	31	61	42
UKAI	66	51	98	104	15	65	25	55	88	103	111	67	31	0	50	31
VALOD	97	19	66	70	34	49	23	52	113	71	113	34	61	50	0	19
VYARA	78	31	78	84	15	61	35	65	95	83	106	62	42	31	19	0
Distances in km.	AHWA	BARDOLI	DUMAS	HAJIRA	KANKRAPAR	KAMREJ	MANDVI	MANGROL	NIJHAR	OLPAD	SAPUTARA	SURAT	UCHCHHAL	UKAI	VALOD	VYARA

SURENDRANAGAR DISTRICT - Distance Chart

	BAMANBORE	CHOTILA	DASADA	DHRANGADHRA	HALVAD	KHARAGHODA	LAKHTAR	LIMDI	MULI	PATDI	SAYALA	SURENDRANAGAR	TARNETAR	THANGADH	WADHWAN	ZINZUVADA
BAMANBORE	0	13	143	91	78	141	100	86	54	131	52	76	40	30	80	156
CHOTILA	13	0	130	78	65	128	87	73	41	118	39	63	27	17	67	163
DASADA	143	130	0	61	88	22	61	94	89	12	101	67	112	147	65	20
DHRANGADHRA	91	78	61	0	27	59	59	62	57	49	69	35	51	61	40	74
HALVAD	78	65	88	27	0	86	86	89	66	76	69	62	38	48	65	101
KHARAGHODA	161	128	22	59	86	0	59	82	77	10	99	65	100	145	63	35
LAKHTAR	100	87	61	59	86	59	0	30	46	49	58	24	114	104	22	74
LIMDI	86	73	94	62	89	82	30	0	46	82	34	27	100	90	22	107
MULI	54	41	89	57	66	77	46	46	0	77	12	37	68	58	25	102
PATDI	131	118	72	49	76	10	49	82	77	0	89	55	100	135	53	25
SAYALA	52	39	101	69	69	99	58	34	12	89	0	34	66	56	37	114
SURENDRANAGAR	76	63	67	35	62	65	24	27	37	55	34	0	90	80	5	80
TARNETAR	40	27	112	51	38	100	114	100	68	100	66	90	0	80	90	125
THANGADH	30	17	147	61	48	145	104	90	58	135	56	80	80	0	80	160
WADHWAN	80	67	65	40	65	63	22	22	25	53	37	5	90	80	0	78
ZINZUVADA	156	143	20	74	101	35	74	107	102	25	114	80	125	160	78	0
Distances in km.	BAMANBORE	CHOTILA	DASADA	DHRANGA-DHRA	HALVAD	KHARA-GHODA	LAKHTAR	LIMDI	MULI	PATDI	SAYALA	SURENDRA-NAGAR	TARNETAR	THANGADH	WADHWAN	ZINZUVADA

VADODARA DISTRICT - Distance Chart

Distances in km.	BODELI	CHANDOD	CHHOTA UDEPUR	DABHOI	JAMBUGAM	KADIPANI	KARJAN	KAYAVAROHAN	NASWADI	PADRA	SHINOR	SAVLI	SANKHEDA	TILAKWADA	VADODARA	VAGHODIA
BODELI	0	61	37	40	5	38	79	50	36	80	88	84	20	48	65	48
CHANDOD	61	0	98	21	66	119	60	41	75	65	69	76	41	22	50	67
CHHOTA UDEPUR	37	98	0	77	32	24	116	97	54	117	125	89	57	78	102	85
DABHOI	40	21	77	0	45	98	39	20	54	44	48	55	20	34	29	46
JAMBUGAM	5	66	32	45	0	38	84	65	41	85	93	89	25	83	53	53
KADIPANI	38	119	24	98	38	0	117	98	34	101	126	127	63	54	127	91
KARJAN	79	60	116	39	84	117	0	19	93	32	47	54	59	73	28	45
KAYAVAROHAN	50	41	97	20	65	98	19	0	74	44	28	55	40	54	29	46
NASWADI	36	75	54	54	41	34	93	74	0	116	102	120	56	20	101	84
PADRA	80	65	117	44	85	101	32	44	116	0	72	41	62	78	15	32
SHINOR	88	69	125	48	93	126	47	28	102	72	0	83	68	82	57	14
SAVLI	84	76	89	55	89	127	54	55	120	41	83	0	66	89	26	36
SANKHEDA	20	41	57	20	25	63	59	40	56	62	68	66	0	54	47	30
TILAKWADA	48	22	78	34	83	54	73	54	20	78	82	89	54	0	63	80
VADODARA	65	50	102	29	53	127	32	29	101	15	57	26	47	63	0	17
VAGHODIA	48	67	85	46	53	41	45	46	84	32	74	36	30	80	17	0

VALSAD & NAVSARI DISTRICT - Distance Chart

Distances in km.	AHWA	BILIMORA	CHIKHLI	DANDI	DHARAMPUR	GANDEVI	NAVSARI	PARDI	SAPUTARA	TITHAL	UBHRAT	UMBERGAON	VALSAD	VANSDA	VAPI	WAGHAI
AHWA	0	97	87	137	82	102	122	122	42	115	142	152	109	46	122	32
BILIMORA	97	0	10	35	39	7	20	46	117	38	40	90	32	51	64	65
CHIKHLI	87	10	0	45	29	15	30	33	107	28	50	84	22	41	50	55
DANDI	137	35	45	0	74	42	15	78	157	74	35	129	68	86	99	105
DHARAMPUR	82	39	29	74	0	44	59	40	102	34	79	70	32	36	40	50
GANDEVI	102	7	15	42	44	0	27	48	122	43	47	99	37	56	65	70
NAVSARI	122	20	30	15	59	27	0	63	142	59	20	114	43	71	41	90
PARDI	122	46	33	78	40	48	63	0	140	15	104	51	13	74	18	88
SAPUTARA	42	117	107	157	102	122	142	140	0	135	162	172	129	66	142	52
TITHAL	115	38	28	74	34	43	59	15	135	0	97	66	4	69	32	83
UBHRAT	142	40	50	35	79	47	20	104	162	97	0	134	73	91	100	110
UMBERGAON	152	94	84	129	70	99	114	51	172	66	134	0	67	106	30	120
VALSAD	109	32	22	68	32	37	43	13	129	4	73	67	0	63	28	77
VANSDA	46	51	41	86	36	56	71	74	66	69	91	106	63	0	76	74
VAPI	122	64	50	99	40	65	81	18	142	32	100	30	28	76	0	90
WAGHAI	32	65	55	105	50	70	90	88	55	83	110	120	77	14	90	0